James 1:5-6

If any of you lacks wisdom, let him ask God, who gives generously to all without reproach, and it will be given him. But let him ask in faith, with no doubting, for the one who doubts is like a wave of the sea that is driven and tossed by the wind.

Exploring Secrets of the Heavenly Realms

Bruce Hines

Exploring Secrets of the Heavenly Realms
Mysteries of the Second Heaven Explained

First Edition,2018
ISBN: 978-1-970062-00-7

Publisher: Kingdom Mysteries Publishing
817 W Park Row, Arlington, TX 76013

Printed in the United States of America

Contents

Foreword

After watching Bruce write this first book in about 3 months, I was initially surprised at how quickly it all came about. Although, as I read through the book, I can personally remember the time frame of each story and each experience. I remember his first encounters with the fallen, when God would send them down to be judged, because we encountered them together. I was there when he received a prophecy from one of our National prophets about how God was going to make known to Bruce the structure of the kingdom of darkness. Because of the vast knowledge that God planned to share with Bruce, I watched and continue to watch, as the Lord drives Bruce to understand each spiritual experience through study, research and cause him to seek out counsel by contacting every person he could find who had true understanding about the fallen. Those specifically who had actually encountered them and who knew of them in the scriptures. I've watched his integrity as he studied to show himself approved before teaching the members of our church and ministry about the fallen. It was 7 years after his first encounter before he spoke publicly about the fallen. This book wasn't written in 3 months, it took over 20 years of combined study and the fruits of experience through healing and deliverance ministry.

Over the years we have prayed for thousands of people suffering from spiritual and emotional wounds, mental issues, as well as demonic complications all the while rejoicing with them in their healing. As we began to understand the structure of the fallen we began to rejoice with families as they were being reconciled and healed after the fallen were judged over the family lines.

If everyone would read and understand Exploring Secrets of the Heavenly Realms, churches, the people in them and their families, our cities, our nations and even our world would change. In Acts 28:27 Luke reminds us of what the prophet Isaiah said in Isaiah 6:9, 10. I pray that you will have the heart to understand, the ears to hear, the eyes to know and be acquainted with the mysteries of the heavenly realms. As you read the rest of this book, you will understand the difference between demons and the fallen.

Leah Ann Hines

Founder and Pastor
Church in One Accord
www.churchinoneaccord.org

Introduction

Throughout Church history, God has used scripture, prophetic words, dreams, and supernatural encounters to give guidance, direction, training, and even warnings to the Church. Those who understood the message, who obeyed, were delivered from all kinds of evil.

Most christian believers talk about or profess to have spiritual authority, yet possess no power, so they really have no authority at all. For most Christians, they lack the knowledge to move in authority. It is one thing to be given authority, and totally another matter in how to operate in authority. When talking about faith, we speak of a faith that is not restricted to a justifying faith, but a faith as a condition of power. Most believers have not looked at faith as the avenue of power. Believer's have heard it preached, but seeking after it requires training. It is my hope to bring to light jurisdictions in the heavenly realms for the purpose of training. The condition of power elevates to offices, spiritual insights, functions, and abilities, for it is impossible to please God or be promoted without exercising faith through power. If we don't know something is there, we can't have faith in that realm. Once we know, we can start to exercise faith through understanding and practical experience to then bring about authority.

There are many things that you will read in this book that are from biblical definition placed in a commentary form, but nothing expounded on as deep as this. I have not found any book that brings forth supernatural events as listed in scripture as the book you are about to read. The things I am writing about are power encounters that I have had according to the scriptures over a 20 year span.

Within the covers of this book you will learn not to attack principalities and powers, called fallen angels, over geographical territories, family bloodlines, and organizations, because it is opening ourselves up to an onslaught of destructive power by evil.

We see that the heavens are ruled by God and the earth belongs to the authority of mankind. The way we operate in the heavens are different than that of the earth. God is the God of the heavens and He alone allocates sovereignty or rights to operate in the cosmos. To operate in the second heavens, there are rules that one must learn and follow. The highest heavens are God's dwelling place, and on His own authority, grants certain members of His family to function in the heavens.

I hope you enjoy the first of at least three books on exploring the heavenly realms and how they operate. As you will see, there are four dimensions to the second heaven, with all classes of angels operating through an administration according to their created number within those four dimensions.

Bruce Hines

Chapter One

Six Steps Demons Seek To Dominate

Having been in ministry for more than 20 years, I have found that most of the body of Christ, including Church leaders, is not equipped nor prepared to deal with demonic manifestations. Most Church leaders and deliverance ministers will simply say not to allow manifestations or demons to speak through the person. Their advice is just telling it to go or that you can become so close to God that it will just leave. Don't believe it!

Do evil spirits just leave? In a small measure, this works after the person repents for sins, renounces legal rights, and breaks curses. There is always a right or reason demons have entered a person's life. My point is that there are many forms to deliverance and exorcism. It should be our will and desire to see individuals set free and released into their spiritual inheritance in Christ Jesus, not debate how ministry is done. A good Church leader will learn the many forms of deliverance and exorcism. They will also understand that demons don't manifest on their own accord, but by the power of the Holy Spirit.

You may be asking what is the difference between deliverance and exorcism. Deliverance from evil spirits happens in most cases from expelling wind through coughing, yawning, sneezing, farting, burping or throwing up. Evil spirits are defined as wind! At times, with weaker evil spirits, the person may feel like something left them. In each case, the person should feel lighter, cleaner or empty. A deliverance happens through non-confrontational or confrontation expulsion. To expel in this way, legal rights or the sins which the person has done; the obedience to the demons temptation by doing or acting sinful, must be repented of and renounced. Curses must also be broken.

Exorcism is when the evil spirit comes up and takes the person over and fights to keep the person through verbal blasphemies, accusations, and supernatural manifestations of all kinds.

Some speak and write about oppression and not demonization or possession. Oppression is nothing more than mental torment because of demon possession. Let's define oppression according to Acts 10:38 which says, "how God anointed Jesus of Nazareth with the Holy Spirit and with great power; and He went around doing good and healing all who were oppressed by the devil, because God was with Him." (AMP) Oppression is to have or exercise power over or to exercise harsh control over one. It means to use one's power against one. The evil spirits use our mental choices, known as free will, against us. It also means to conquer and to be enslaved, even to be treated as a slave. This is mental torment and possession!

Again, what does that spiritually mean, to use one's power against one? It means that evil is to put such pressure through the sinful nature that the person uses the power of free will to choose evil, invoking a contract or marriage with those evil spirits. This comes from inside. The feeling is internal. If you think about how Israel was enslaved to the taskmasters of Egypt, you can picture oppression. The oppressed person is possessed and is now under the control of the evil spirits through willful choice. Those evil spirits conquered the will in that area and now seek to set up a stronghold to fortify their sphere to influence behavior. Again, to be oppressed is to be subdued. What does that mean, conquered, overcome, trounced, and crushed. Until the stronghold is firmly established, the sin or legal entry of the possessed person plays on their passions, desires, and thoughts. Giving into sexual immorality, anger, rejection, drugs or alcohol and other sins.

I know that some will say that possession is not biblical, but possession is demonization. Evil spirits have gained legal precedence or seniority over a part of the person through willful sin or contract of sin. In other words, sinful behavior leads to contractual arrangements with evil and some

DELIVERANCE HAPPENS THROUGH NON-CONFRONTATIONAL OR CONFRONTATION EXPULSION.

biblical definitions define it as a marriage contract. Evil spirits seek to dominate the will of humanity.

Have you ever been around believers who confront Satan directly, saying that they belong to Christ Jesus and that the devil does not have any power? These believers slander angelic majesties and violate God's word which warns against doing such things. These believers fail to understand what is actually saved, what must be renewed, and what is dead because of sin. Evil spirits tempt, but it is the free choice of the person that decides freedom or demonization.

James 1:13-15 tells us simply how the kingdom of darkness gains access to our lives.

> *Let no one say when he is tempted, "I am being tempted by God" [for temptation does not originate from God, but from our own flaws]; for God cannot be tempted by [what is] evil, and He Himself tempts no one. But each one is tempted when he is dragged away, enticed and baited [to commit sin] by his own [worldly] desire (lust, passion). Then when the illicit desire has conceived, it gives birth to sin; and when sin has run its course, it gives birth to death. (AMP)*

Let no one say when he is tempted, "I am tempted by God"; for God cannot be tempted by evil, nor does He Himself tempt anyone. But each one is tempted when he is drawn away by his own desires and enticed. Then, when desire has conceived, it gives birth to sin; and sin, when it is full-grown, brings forth death. (NKJV)

The Bible clearly points to the origin of temptation, the sinful nature. From the old man, the satanic nature, temptation looks to enter mankind. The nature of fallen humanity, the flesh of mankind is satanic and sinful. It is rebellious in its function and desires. Romans 6:20 (AMP) says temptation comes from our flawed nature.

"When you were slaves of sin, you were free in regard to righteousness [you had no desire to conform to God's will]." Notice, no desire to obey God's will. That is the nature of Satan, a rebel to the core. So when we feel like rebelling, that is the old self that still belongs to the kingdom of darkness. It is that transaction that Adam made with the devil, and its evil nature is rebellious at heart. Yet God's plan is to replace the old self with the new self, the born-again nature, the nature of Christ Jesus.

So the first step to demons dominating someone's life is temptation. Temptation means to be tested or to be evaluated. This is why Satan asked for Peter to be sifted as wheat. Temptation should be evaluated by weight or load. What is spiritually happening? The person being tempted by evil is being put to the test in order to ascertain the imperfections or faults in the nature as to be possessed. What does that mean? The kingdom of darkness is seeking information in an attempt to learn something by careful investigation or searching through the person's nature. Simply put, the character of someone is being examined and tested for failure. Our life and how we live it reflects which nature is in control and how much of each nature belongs to which kingdom. The old man can't help but sin and the new man cannot sin. 1 John 5:4 says, "whatever is born of God overcomes the world." 1 John 3:9 says, "whoever has been born of God does not sin, for His (God's) seed remains in him; and he cannot sin, because he has been born of God." So we see, God does not tempt!

EVIL SPIRITS TEMPT, BUT IT IS THE FREE CHOICE OF THE PERSON THAT DECIDES FREEDOM OR DEMONIZATION.

The second step James says is to be carried away. It is by a lust or desire, or craving in the sinful nature, that causes a person to be lured away. It means to draw out and remove. When the person is tempted, the second part starts. Temptation or that impulse activates a desire or craving inside the emotions, a feeling to have, and so we feel it in the body, the old man, the brokenness. It is like a fish being lured by a fishing lure or bait to be caught. At this point the demons are sifting, examining, testing for willful entry. Demons tempt and prey on the sinful nature, to get the person to willfully surrender so that they may enter through contract. Notice the Amplified Bible says to be baited to commit sin by the person's own worldly or carnal desire through different kinds of lusts and passions that are contrary to God's word. So at this point, the evil spirits have only tested for failure, yet have not gained legal entry or possession.

The third step is demonization! Enticed means to cause someone to sin or enticed to sin. This is the legal right to enter the person. Evil spirits come in at this point. It means to catch by bait through being deceived. The person has been seduced by evil spirits to sin. The definition sense is to greatly desire to do and to have the person in reference to the entity or spirit through event for a state.

Now, the evil spirits have the legal right to parts of the person's soul through willful choice and integrate themselves in that person's emotions, looking for the power of choice of the human will, emotions, mind or thought patterns. The evil spirits must govern the willful choice of the person. So they seek to establish control over the emotions to weaken the will of the person. This is how evil spirits start to dominate the mind. So, recapping legal entry, the person becomes beguiled or charmed in a deceptive way. To be dazzled or bewitched through a spell to win over by act of teasing or flattery. Yes, the person is seduced to sin!

The fourth step is conception! James says, "Then when the illicit desire has conceived." This is illegal behavior, according to the laws of God's word. Conceived means to become pregnant. This means on the outside at the start, things look to be normal. But over time that sin starts to

THEIR GOAL OR END PRODUCT IS TO HAVE COMPLETE CONTROL OVER THAT PART OF YOU.

seize the person's behavior as that sin starts to grow. The evil spirits start to slowly take control through the mind, will, and emotions as stated before. The definition means to become pregnant or undergo change; to essentially turn through change. I call this stage, the development or steps in a process of secret sin. This is where the battle on the inside for the will of the human starts to become more intense. The evil spirits on the inside seek to wear down the individual until they give in and choose to surrender. They yield their mind, will, and emotions over so that a stronghold can be built.

There are signs of demonic possession, like, why am I starting to feel sad or depressed? Why am I struggling with anger or rejection? Why do my finances come and go? Why are there so many things that are going bad in my life all of a sudden? Why do the same situations keep happening to me? Understanding the process of spiritual warfare answers the classic age old question, "why do bad things happen to good people?" The simplest answer, bad things happen if the devil has the right to make them happen. The fallen angels have demons assigned to look for legal rights to attack you and to bring people into bondage.

Let us break that down! Are you a Christian and are you living an on going sanctified lifestyle? Or, is the world engaged as much or more than Christ Jesus? Have you broke generational curses? Curses are evil in the bloodline and are passed down from generation to generation until broken. Remember, each curse must be undone in accordance with the way in which it was done. If the curse was witchcraft in origin, then witchcraft must be renounced. Has there been abuse in your life? Unresolved abusive trauma that must go through inner-healing? Without inner healing most legal rights and curses cannot be broken. What kind of relationships have you had or are you seeking?

How do I know if I have a curse and a legal right for evil spirits to do bad things to me? It is the measurement of something and degree of something formula? The standard or caliber or the measure of the badness of the bad things that have happened and the amount of the bad things that have happened indicate whether it is a curse. Legal rights and curses usually start with willful or deliberate acts of sin. Also, through inadvertent or accidental sinful acts. Generational curses are very powerful to bring about destruction.

One of the most active spirits of this age is Jezebel. This spirit will destroy your health, your finances, your marriage, and family. Jezebel is all about murder and blood sacrifice. This is the foundation that Jezebel works off of. Wherever there is Jezebel, there are Lucifer and Lilith.

The fifth step in demon domination is, it gives birth to sin. The will of the demons start to be seen by people. It can no longer be hidden, it has become a vice. This is where the vice becomes a stronghold and is becoming out of control. The demonized person starts to produce fruit for the kingdom of darkness. This is where the person starts to leave bread crumbs of sin that can be traced. This is where the person is caught in sin like below, and is sorrowful but not repentant. They promise not to do it again, but yet again they fall short. Galatians 5:19-21 lists some of the fruit.

> *"Now the practices of the sinful nature are clearly evident: they are sexual immorality, impurity, sensuality (total irresponsibility, lack of self- control), idolatry, sorcery, hostility, strife, jealousy, fits of anger, disputes, dissensions, factions [that promote heresies], envy, drunkenness, riotous behavior, and other things like these. I warn you beforehand, just as I did previously, that those who practice such things will not inherit the kingdom of God." (AMP)*

As you read my chapter on strongholds I will make it clearer, but for now, imply understand that a stronghold is brought out into the open. Just as a baby grows from childbirth, so now the stronghold grows and is increasing in size and strength. James says the final step is to accomplish or to bring to completion what was started and desired in the beginning. What the evil spirits desired from the beginning when the temptation came, to finish. Their goal or end product is to have complete control over that part of you. Their will is now your will because they have embedded themselves so deep in the mind, will, and emotions that exorcism is the only way to freedom. The addictive behavior, like drugs can't be removed. The person can dry out. They can even go through the physical withdrawal, but the minute they're around that stronghold again, they return to the mud like the pig. For example behavior like anger, those explosive people, anger with an edge, that is demon domination. James says it brings forth death. Demons kill, steal, and destroy. These are proven steps that I have ministered to thousands of people so that they can come to the understanding of demon domination. The Bible is full of secrets hidden in plain sight!

Chapter Two

Strongholds

First, before anything else, we must be able to define and understand how strongholds work, only then can a stronghold be attacked and pulled down. We must remember that strongholds are how demons stay in control; whereas legal rights are how demons enter the human body for possession or demonization. One more thing before we move on, possession means to take possession or to seize or to inherit or impoverish. When demons come in and take possession it is due to an area of one's life which has been surrendered to sin and now those spirits consider that person's body their property and guard it as a military fortification or stronghold.

POSSESSION IS DUE TO AN AREA OF ONE'S LIFE WHICH HAS BEEN SURRENDERED TO SIN.

There are three sides or steps to a stronghold described by Paul in 2 Corinthians 10:3-6. The first side or foundation of a stronghold is knowledge. So the first step of a demonic stronghold is false knowledge or belief in a lie. The second step is imaginations or arguments, reasoning. We argue or reason in our minds over the truth or over supernatural manifestation. We choose to not recognize or don't know scriptural truth, so we believe what we want to believe based upon our own understanding, this is a stronghold. There is a consideration or reasoning if we are going to choose truth or lie. Arguments always lead to thoughts which are the third side or step to a stronghold. These thoughts are the content of what the person is thinking about and arguing with, what to choose to believe; I call them a series of thoughts to justify action or belief. For instance, when a person possessed believes a lie, then that person speaks or acts according to that lie. The person either does not know the truth of scripture or has been told by someone or the demons a lie about themselves or what they are witnessing. Once we believe the lie, actions start to take place. These actions are seen in behavior that cannot be corrected. It doesn't matter how hard the person tries, things like sexual immorality, fear, hatred, self-hatred, idolatry, anger, depression, addiction, abuse, rejection, racial prejudice, religious superstition and many others seem to drive that person's behavior. So we live from a realm of false knowledge, arguing against the truth, and our thoughts lead us to justify our false beliefs and actions.

ONCE WE BELIEVE THE LIE, ACTIONS START TO TAKE PLACE.

The real power of demonic possession is when evil takes control of our emotions. Evil spirits want us to believe that it is we who are angry or looking at pornography or feeling sexual desires, but it is really the demon of anger, porn or immorality who has meshed or merged or weaved themselves into who we are emotionally and then influences our feelings and desires to stay in control of our personality and actions. This bad behavior will continue because evil spirits have legal rights, curses, and strongholds in our life and the goal is to make bad things happen to us. What I am saying is that strongholds are visible deliberate sinful acts that seem unintended or unplanned or desired. Often you see these behaviors repeated in families, this reveals a curse and a stronghold. I like to refer to them as "iniquities of the fathers".

Let us look at Acts 19:11-20 and see from scripture what a stronghold looks like. Again we see that strongholds are felt or sensed through sinful desires, and it is our choices and our actions that reveals the type of strongholds that are present.

The scene is set; the power of the Holy Spirit was doing unusual or extraordinary miracles through Paul, these miracles were special, even remarkable. The handkerchiefs or face towels and aprons that had touched the skin of Paul were brought to the sick and the people's diseases left them. We should notice two things, one is divine healing, but the second is that the Bible makes note of sickness leaving or departing the people; this is deliverance for healing. Spirits of infirmity were leaving, but also evil demonic spirits were being expelled or cast out. It was not the towel or apron; it was not Paul's anointing, it was God working. The definition of disease here is a state of physical incapacity or illness, usually as the result of a controlling supernatural force. This is a stronghold of sickness.

It must have been a powerful movement of God because when the Jewish exorcists, who do exorcism according to the Law of Moses. As followers of the Old Testament covenant they attempted to proclaim the name of the Lord Jesus over the evil spirit by verbalizing a command and by ordering the spirit to leave the person. The spirit speaks to the exorcists. This is a stronghold. The spirit came up in the man, spoke through the man's voice and started a legal conversation and process. Demonic spirits only recognize spiritual authority. Just a quick note. The reason why the demon attacked them is that they were trying to operate out of a different covenant.

During an exorcism or deliverance the person is sometimes conscious or awake as the spirit speaks, and other times completely unaware, remembering nothing of the event. The Bible does not tell us if the man was completely taken over or that he was aware that he was possessed and the spirit working through his will showing dominion over character, but simply that the demon spoke.

DEMONIC SPIRITS ONLY RECOGNIZE SPIRITUAL AUTHORITY.

This demon said he knew and recognized Jesus' authority, he even knew Paul, and that is to say the evil spirit respected Paul and how God was working through him in the region. But these exorcists were not worshipers and followers of Jesus Christ and had no spiritual authority according to New Testament covenant. The covenant that gives its believers authority and power as followers of Jesus. We have seen how the evil spirit took control of the mind and spoke through the person, now we see the spirit take control of the emotions and thoughts and leap upon or attack the seven men. He sprung up, presumably from a seated position and overpowered seven men. With vengeance, the demon overpowered them, and sent them running naked from the house. This is a stronghold! The demon was able to bypass the will of the person, taking charge of the persons mind, and stimulating the man's emotions so that his thoughts and feelings were intent on doing harm. The emotions became so intense, that he violently attacked them.

This process begins with willful surrender and then yielding to the thoughts that the demon is emotionally stirring up. In this example the demon, through the man, sought injury, therefore, it is possible this demon was stirring up thoughts of anger, rage, hatred and malice. This is what demons do; they look to master the person by gaining dominion and control of the mind, will, and emotions to exercise complete control over the person's life. Have you ever seen a Christian or pastor commit sexual immorality, adultery, lie, steal, use drugs or is angry? It makes you wonder, who is that really? You thought that the person you knew would have never done such horrible things. I believe the flesh gets blamed far too much for behavior that continues to be unresponsive to godliness.

The will is the place of choice. A person who is drug addicted has a fleshy craving, and thoughts continually invade the mind and begin to wear down the willful choice leading them to believe that they need the drug. The human craving is from the demons who consider our body their house to do their will. The desires that fuel the thoughts are from the demons, and all is from false knowledge. Until the person uses their will to overcome drugs or is put in a position where the drugs are unavailable, only then will the power of the demons be broken as the body purifies itself and the will of the person is strengthened and taught to no longer choose drugs.

The legal right that brought the demons in for possession and the stronghold they have set up still exists within the mind, will, emotions and body of that person. This is why someone could go years drug free or sexually pure, but the minute they are exposed to that sin or the stronghold inside them, that temptation, empowered through that unresolved stronghold, becomes active again. In consequence the emotional desire or temptation to sin reveals the strength of the stronghold. If the demons are not expelled, they will continue to work through thoughts, and create desires so that the person enters that vice again, and so becomes enslaved all over again.

From the first chapter of the gospel of Mark we learn that demons never work alone. There is never just one demon assigned to guard a fortress or stronghold, but many! Yet, there is one chief or strongman over that stronghold. Mark 1:21-28 reveals that ministry should happen as believers assemble and worship the Lord. Capernaum was a town with wealth as well as sin, depravity with self-indulgence.

DEMONS LOOK TO MASTER THE PERSON BY GAINING DOMINION AND CONTROL OF THE MIND, WILL, AND EMOTIONS.

The Bible says that Jesus began to teach, imparting skills and knowledge, and the crowd was astonished. The Greek word astonished is an extremely strong word and could also be translated amazed or astounded. It also has a meaning, "to strike out, expel by a blow, drive out or away, to strike one out of self-possession". Yes Jesus was explaining how the Kingdom of God has come to invade this evil age with authority and power, to bring redemption to all mankind and deliverance from demonic spirits and His powerful message caused demons and evil spirits to be revealed. The definition indicates the Lord's message was a discourse of some length. This pattern continues, when Jesus preached, demonic activity reveals itself and Jesus asserts His authority by casting it out. What an impact Jesus made, teaching about God's saving grace in himself, Christ, and authority over evil spirits and sickness, he imparted knowledge and skills to overcome this evil age empowered by sin.

We see again in the first chapter of Mark, as in Acts 19, that a demonic spirit is speaking out of a man. The evil spirit had enough control of the person's mind to speak through him. The unclean spirit was able to manifest through the man's emotions and speak through his will. In other words, the character of the evil spirit was using the man's mind and body to do and say something. This man was living under a sphere or power of the demons control; they considered this man's body, their home. In the NASB the demon says to Jesus, "what business do you have with us?" Notice one demon speaking for many under his command. This is why I cast out not only the demon speaking, but all who work for him. Remember the fact that the demons have no rest or control over humanity unless they are living in someone's physical body.

This word business has to do with a reference to receiving of a message. This message of this evil age is sin! Essentially what the demon is saying to Jesus is, "This man listened to my message, acted on my message and gave me and other evil spirits legal right to enter him and to set up a stronghold. What right do you have to this man?" What does the kingdom of darkness have in common with you and the kingdom of light? Kingdoms declare a message and it all comes down to which message we want to live under. The one demon speaking for those under him cried out or screamed. The demon cried out, using the man's vocal organs. It was a deep, from the throat, terrible cry, but in defiance, claiming legal rights and curses which allow his stronghold and the right to control. In other words, "This man is our property!"

There is a large amount of confusion over what is meant by the word rebuke. Most believers say that Jesus rebuked evil spirits, and they came out, and this is true, but the definition and meaning go deeper. There is more here than meets the eye. The rebuke is to the demons for failing to acknowledge sin by the message He was proclaiming to this man and all mankind. Jesus reproved and scolded the demons for their wrong, revealing their legal rights, strongholds and curses, and overcame them with His message. In deliverance language, Jesus rebuked every single lie the demons had the man believing and preached His message of truth. This man must have heard and believed the message of truth Jesus preached, because the demons came out of him. What is not mentioned in the scripture are two examples, is that there must have been repentance, forgiveness, renunciation, curse breaking, and honesty for the demons to leave.

One more thing here, Jesus commanded the demon to be quiet. This means the demon was saying more than just acknowledging Jesus as Messiah and that Jesus needed the demon to be quiet to proceed. I find this to be very true! Most of the time the demon is talking through thought to the person being delivered, lying to them, trying to make them believe something that is false so the demon doesn't have to go. So I command the demon to be muzzled or remain speechless. No longer do I allow the demons to speak to the person through the mind or by any voice while being delivered. I tell them to speak to me directly and lie not to the Holy Spirit.

> **I CAST OUT NOT ONLY THE DEMON SPEAKING, BUT ALL WHO WORK FOR HIM.**

This exorcism account in Mark's gospel indicates that a chief or resident demon affects not only the thinking and words but also the physical behavior of a host. When Jesus rebukes the demon it causes the man to convulse and cry out again. The reason for the second cry is all his rights and their stronghold to be in the body have been removed, so the demon and those who work for him are calling out for help so that they don't have to leave. The convulsion means to rend, tear and shake uncontrollably. If the demon can rend or split the soul, they will not have to come out totally or fully, but only give up some ground. This is not an external slit or cut, but an internal rip or slash of the mind. Command the demons not to rend or tear and convulse not, but to come out.

To be a good deliverance minister we must think legally, using God's word as the law of the universe and enforcing the law of God. Demons use the breaking of God's law to gain legal right and possession in our life. Repentance is a firm mind set on turning away from sin and living a life in pursuit of holiness. When we forgive, God freely forgives us of all our sins, so we confess our sin, so we can be set free. This is how we stay free of demon possession. We renounce our sins and transgressions and break all curses activated by sin. We also must be humble and honest, going to those dark places that have hurt and pain and unpleasant memories, so that we can receive inner healing.

The Church must realize that there is a contest between light and darkness in which each endeavors to throw the other down, and which is decided when the victor is able to press and hold down his opponent face down, and to hold him down with his hand upon his neck rendering the opponent helpless. We live in an age between Jesus' showdown in the wilderness and His second coming. Jesus' purpose was to take on the powers of darkness, defeat them, and offer mankind eternal redemption. This is why believers must be trained in deliverance. This is the only ministry that is called on to confront the powers of darkness to bring breakthrough.

In Luke 13:10-17 a woman had an illness for eighteen years, which is the biblical number for bondage, and the illness was caused by a demon spirit of infirmity. She was bent over or double, facing her feet, and she could not straighten up at all. This demon spirit was a demon who caused sickness. The textual language indicates that this woman entered the synagogue while Jesus was teaching. However she got there, it must have come from a deep desire to be set free. Most in the Church don't understand that to have an illness that incapacitates or is life threatening, comes from an evil spirit of infirmity. The definition in her deliverance has to do with divorce, pardon and release. From the definition, there must have been some type of contractual rights that had been concealed. Vows and oaths play a big part in contracts with the devil as do ceremonies and rituals. Notice Jesus pardoned her or loosed (released) her, she was freed. This is a courtroom decision based on her response to the knowledge and skills, the way to be freed or healed.

THERE IS A CONTEST BETWEEN LIGHT AND DARKNESS IN WHICH EACH ENDEAVORS TO THROW THE OTHER DOWN.

We have been talking about how demons work through the human mind called strongholds. But everyone must understand that demons are evil personalities, spirit beings without bodies. These demonic personalities are a set of characteristics, the totality of attitudes, interests, behavioral patterns and emotional responses. This is what works inside the human mind when demon possession has occurred. Demons partner with human personalities to influence a course of thinking and beliefs. Demons become so one with the person that even the body responds. Let me give you an example. If we hurt a part of our body due to an accident; in our mind we feel the pain, so it is with demon possession. If there is a spirit of lust inside, there is an overwhelming feeling in the body through the thought of lust and a desire or craving to give the body the lust that it wants. So we see the demons desires of lust working through the mind and emotions of man.

Demons are spirit beings. Demonic spirits seek to tempt, deceive, condemn, defile, control, afflict with disease, kill, and destroy, and the like. There is always an open door or legal right for demons to enter the person's life, and then the person becomes demonized; but strongholds are worked out as the human will surrenders to the thoughts and desires based on false knowledge of the demons in the flesh or body.

In Matthew 16:21-23, we see another form of a stronghold revealed. Peter shortly after disclosing that Jesus is the Christ, the Messiah, made known to Peter by God the Father. Peter comes under a different influence as Jesus reveals God's plan. As Peter was listening to the truth, Jesus clearly revealing the Father's plan, and the suffering that would be paid for the redemption of mankind, the devil then speaks through Peters mind through thoughts. In this private conversation Peter starts to reprimand Jesus. Peter's thoughts and his reasoning start to express strong disapproval with God's plan. Jesus quickly discerned that Peter's mind was being used by Satan. Moments before, God the Father was revealing Jesus the Messiah to Peter's mind in such a way that it caused Peter to speak and confess Jesus the Christ. Now the devil steps into Peter's mind and tries to use their relationship to create a trap. We call these traps stumbling blocks, they are designed to cause you to sin. It is anything that causes or intends a person to sin whether by preventing righteous actions or by promoting sinful behavior. Peter's problem, he was not dwelling on the things Jesus just explained, but turned his mind over to the things of man and so the devil stepped in and spoke through Peter to Jesus. The truth of God's plan was to cause Peter and the disciples to be set free or to be released from a way of thinking. The point here is once the stronghold is pulled down, the mind is free to accept the truth and bring freedom to the soul.

SATAN DOES NOT WANT US TO UNDERSTAND THE LAWS TO SPIRITUAL WARFARE.

Jesus spent much of His earthly ministry dealing with the devil and bringing to light principles of spiritual warfare. How can we expect to have victory over the kingdom of darkness if we don't deal with evil spirits and understand how they work? It is important as Revelation 2:24 says, to know the deep things of Satan, otherwise the Bible would remain silent concerning the ways of darkness.

Satan does not want us to understand the laws to spiritual warfare. Most believers think that the devil and the kingdom of evil have been defeated, yet these evil spirits are at work today. Yes Jesus defeated them, which now gives us the right to go out and defeat them as well. To take what has been given through the cross and exercise it when sin is involved.

Another Christian saying is Jesus took away all the armor in which Satan trusts, yet there are evil spirits who have the armor of Satan. The limitations of the kingdom of darkness all depends on an individual believer who is operating in spiritual law. So the forces of darkness can do only what each individual believer lawfully allows them to do.

Chapter Three

Curses

What is a curse? A curse, according to Louw-Nida (Biblical Definer), is to cause injury or harm by means of a statement [words, which are acts] regarded as having some supernatural power, often because a deity [fallen angel] or supernatural force [demon] has been invoked. The words in parentheses are mine. Very few authors really write the deep spiritual truths about curses. There seems to be a fear of being so forthright. I think it is time to be direct and honest. In this chapter, we will talk about the difference between fallen angels and demons. Yet my next book about the fallen angels will be just as direct and as honest. The Dictionary of New Testament Theology states that a curse is a malediction [slander], and in ancient thought, the spoken word had intrinsic power, which was released by the act of utterance. The person cursed was thus exposed to a sphere of destructive power. It worked effectively against a person until the power of the curse was broken.

Notice that power is found within the curse and thus, the curse itself must be broken. In my reduced definition, a curse starts with words and behaviors, while evil spirits are attached to the words to empower the curse. So curses are words or actions that call on an evil spirit on any level to perform a function. The curse is then a function. The evil spirit has a function or assignment. This assignment comes with what is said and or done. Fallen angels in the celestial realm or demons in the terrestrial realm need words or actions for legal rights. In most cases, demons use actions for legal rights. Curses or evil spirits with assignments have their origin in sin. A curse or an evil spirit with a function is one of the most powerful weapons the kingdom of darkness uses against mankind. If you noticed, a curse operates on whatever level in the celestial realm, and whatever level in the terrestrial realm. These evil spirits with functions, also recognized as the power within a curse, must have a legal right to land or enter the person. A curse or evil spirit enters the family bloodline to carry out its assignment until someone breaks the curse through words of renunciation. These evil assignments destroy our future. They slow us down and work against our calling and our level of success.

CURSES ARE WORDS OR ACTIONS THAT CALL ON AN EVIL SPIRIT ON ANY LEVEL TO PERFORM A FUNCTION.

So all these curses will come on you and pursue you and overtake you until you are destroyed because you would not obey the voice of the Lord your God by keeping His commandments and His statutes which He has commanded you. (Deuteronomy 28:45 AMP)

We can see four functions or assignments that an evil spirit tries to accomplish through supernatural power against the person.

First, a curse shall come upon you. That means an evil spirit will enter you with a specific assignment, and will aggressively seek to carry out that assignment. These evil spirits will be relentless in nature, constantly oppressing someone through possession, as heat oppresses on a hot summer day.

The second function of an evil spirit with a curse is that it pursues. It pursues its assignment until they are subdued or overtaken. Its main purpose for existence is to destroy!

The third reason evil spirits are so fervent about pursuing their assignments is that they receive supernatural power if they complete their function or assignment in each generation. In other words, each assignment completed against a generation brings more spiritual power over the next generation. Addictive behavior, seen in alcoholism in one generation, evolves into drug addiction in the next generation. Divorce in one generation evolves into giving birth to children outside of wedlock. What happens is that curses become more powerful and lives are destroyed, purposes and destinies are lost, and family legacies are wiped out. A curse is a function, with different levels of power of an evil spirit, period. That function will continue until the curse is broken and the spirits are expelled.

Lastly, a curse can only be broken with words which undo the assignment. Breaking the agreement with the evil spirit assigned to the words and action is the only recourse. It is the New Testament instruction for curses. The function, that was invoked by some word or deed, must be undone or reversed by repenting and renouncing the curse, then expelling the demon and those who work under it.

ALCOHOLISM IN ONE GENERATION, EVOLVES INTO DRUG ADDICTION IN THE NEXT GENERATION

I will say it again, expulsion through deliverance is the person's best option. Just renouncing through revelatory gifting helps, but we can only see and know in part. A curse is a legally binding document or contract in the spirit world with an evil spirit. The person binds not only themselves but binds future generations to the pact or agreement. Each level of curses has its rules of engagement. For example, the way you handle a demon may not be the same way you handle a demonic strongman. This also applies when dealing with fallen angels, who sired the demons.

Whether it is the court of heaven or non-confrontational deliverance, the only way to make sure everything is gone is by undergoing confrontational deliverance. This has been my finding after witnessing and performing ten thousand terrestrial deliverances and about one thousand celestial deliverances. I would be glad to sit down with someone who has had the same experiences I have to discuss differing options.

Here is my point, power must be in the now or its only theory. What do I mean by 'power must be in the now'? What I mean is that if you only do non-confrontational or revelatory deliverance, you will leave the next generation with bloodline issues.

Let me give an example – If someone in your family line has been involved in the occult or sought out cultic shamans, like those in the new age movement, everything the shaman did and everything said must be specifically renounced. Because differing ceremonies contain different rituals, the words spoken and acts done in that specific ritual must be renounced in reverse order to break the contract. One definition defines expel or cast out as being bound by an oath! Let me say this! All forms of deliverance are valuable, and all forms of deliverance are necessary!

Words are powerful in the spirit realm. Life and death lie in the power of the tongue! Confrontational or non-confrontational deliverance is the biblical procedure for casting out demons.

POWER MUST BE IN THE NOW OR ITS ONLY THEORY.

For fallen angels in the celestial realms, the legal rights are completely different than those of demons. Demonic legal rights are tied to spoken words and deeds. However, with fallen angels, their legal rights have to do with the mindset of humanity and families. These legal rights are laws humans live under that transgress God's law. Mankind calls their laws right, but they are in fact violated statues; broken covenants between God and mankind.

When dealing with fallen angels in the second heaven, there must be a court case in which the individual's case must be argued in the courtroom of heaven. Yes, I said argued! Anyone who has dealt with fallen angels successfully, and has seen families go through deliverance all at once knows this to be true. Just like in our human courts, the case must be argued, a verdict must be reached that leads to a sentence or judgment, and then finally there must be incarceration.

> *So he sent messengers to Balaam the son of Beor, at Pethor, which is near the River, in the land of the sons of his people, to call him, saying, "Behold, a people came out of Egypt; behold, they cover the surface of the land, and they are living opposite me. Now, therefore, please come, curse these people for me since they are too mighty for me; perhaps I may be able to defeat them and drive them out of the land. For I know that he whom you bless is blessed, and he whom you curse is cursed." (Numbers 22:5-6 NASB)*

Notice the reason an evil spirit was called upon to perform a function, was in order to destroy Israel with a curse. King Balak saw that Israel was too strong for them, both supernaturally and in military might. He needed someone who could conjure up powerful evil spirits to destroy Israel. Like Jannes and Jambress opposed Moses, Balak sought after a prophetic sorcerer named Balaam – A prophetic diviner who could call upon high fallen angels to cast destructive supernatural power over a people group. (This ability to control the rights of entire people groups is one of the assignments of the fallen angels.) Balak needed someone who could prophetically discern the atmosphere; someone who could summon the different levels and sublevels of the fallen angel structure in that region. It had to be an evil prophetic word with dimensions, thrones, dominions, principalities or powers attached to it, one that could handle the assignment. Balaam would spiritually engage darkness and then speak curses according to the fallen angel's voice. This is what was going on in Numbers 22.

From many of my own observations, sorcerers who are good enough at tapping into the spirit realm in order to get their tasks done may have gifts that could be used by God. Yes, you read that correctly. All gifts come from Him. God can use their gift to bless, but not in the normal way a believer might think of blessing.

TAKE BACK CITIES, REGIONS, STATES, AND NATIONS BY TAKING THE GOSPEL INTO THESE REGIONS.

Let me give an example: I knew a lesbian woman who would get high on marijuana and have her cards read. She came from a Christian family, but generational curses and childhood abuse sent her down a road of destruction. There were curses with evil spirits assigned to her that were trying to kill her through suicide. The last time she had her cards read in this state, she said, "God, I want to know the truth." The medium she was visiting told her that she had a family reunion coming up she should attend, but warned her that something would try to stop her from going. The medium said she must go despite the resistance because whatever she was looking for would be there. At her family reunion, the woman's aunt was there and had the chance to speak to her about the Holy Spirit and introduced her to a deliverance minister. The medium had no idea that God was guiding this suffering woman to Himself through her actions. This is not a normal procedure by any means, but God the Father is ruler over all. She accepted Jesus just days later! Today, after 57 demonic exorcisms and 11 fallen angel deliverances, she is preaching the gospel and is powerful in the Holy Spirit and His gifts.

To recognize evil spirits working through curses in the family bloodlines, look for devastating patterns of sin, poverty, sickness, mental issues, and accidents with medical bills. What is your family line called to? God seeks godly children through righteous bloodlines. Each family line has callings, gifts, and purposes connected to it, to further the Kingdom of God. Each generation is not meant to battle for what the fathers already attained. Children are never meant to battle for what their fathers already worked for, the successes, achievements, and revelations about the spirit realm. It should be passed down from generation to generation. Parents should pass on business, finances, and spiritual secrets to the Kingdom of God. Let's look at Timothy in the New Testament!

> *I remember your sincere and unqualified faith [the surrendering of your entire self to God in Christ with confident trust in His power, wisdom, and goodness, a faith] which first lived in [the heart of] your grandmother Lois and your mother Eunice, and I am confident that it is in you as well. That is why I remind you to fan into flame the gracious gift of God, [that inner fire—the special endowment] which is in you through the laying on of my hands [with those of the elders at your ordination]. (2 Timothy 1:5-6 Amplified Bible)*

Timothy inherited so much faith through his bloodline that God connected him to Paul the Apostle. Notice that Timothy was, at minimum, a third generation believer in God. This is important! There is spiritual power that can be tapped into and then released from generational Christians. Many parents that are believers fail to train their children, in order to pass on spiritual gifts and callings. God paired Timothy and Paul so that Timothy could carry the next wave of Christianity to his generation.

However, we see that Timothy had a spirit of fear, also known as a curse. This fear was the function of an evil spirit, which probably stemmed from a generational curse, seeing as fear is a root spirit in the Bible. The function of this fear was to make Timothy timid, in order to supernaturally

WHEN WE FOCUS ON HEAVEN'S AGENDA, GOD SHIFTS THE SECOND HEAVEN.

block him from the realm of faith and stop him from operating in signs and wonders. This fear was a generational issue – one that had been passed on to him through his bloodline. When the Apostle Paul identified this in Timothy, he called the spirit of fear a demon! Timothy must have been delivered from it, seeing as he ministered with and served the Apostle Paul to the end of his life.

Some people teach that we can go into the courts of heaven and deal with curses over cities, regions, states or nations. This is just not true! Legal rights come from sin, but territorial sins are strongholds. You can pray in the courts for an outpouring of the spirit, but you take back cities, regions, states, and nations by taking the gospel into these regions. We are to go with the gifts of the Holy Spirit to weaken the fallen angels. Why? God's power falls, people are saved, demons are cast out, and healings breakout. This is biblical training – even Jesus dealt with the devil in the terrestrial realm. Jesus has me deal with fallen angels in the terrestrial realm. God actually sends them down for judgment. Why? The gospel is being preached. Demons are being cast out. The healing of the sick is taking place. God is waiting for humanity to take back the earth. When we focus on heaven's agenda, God shifts the second heaven.

The Bible clearly teaches in 1 John 3:8 that the devil has been sinning from the beginning. What does that say to me? The fallen angels who rule over this evil age are the authors of sin. Sin is in every human being. We call it the flesh. So through the carnal nature, the fallen angels have rights and or potential access. That is why we are to put off the old man and put on the new man, made in the likeness of Jesus. Let us look at a scripture in the book of John.

You belong to your father, the devil, and you want to carry out your father's desires. He was a murderer from the beginning, not holding to the truth, for there is no truth in him. When he lies, he speaks his native language, for he is a liar and the father of lies (John 8:44 NIV).

Jesus says that the devil and the fallen angels are the authors (or fathers) over the fleshly nature. Notice, I group all the Fallen together; combat has taught me that. Within that fleshly nature is the satanic principal, whose chief goal is to carry out the desires of evil angels. These are bloodline curses and generational strongholds in the heavenly realms. When fallen angels speak to humanity, it is through lies, division, and deception. The core nature of fallen angels is not only one of lies and deception, but of murder: killing off bloodlines from the beginning. Here's the key: there is no truth in fallen angels or demons, so we the Church are to take the truth to a deceived world.

Chapter Four

The Armor Of Satan

I will give a brief introduction leading up to our text, Luke 11:20-23. Verse 14 shows us when Jesus was driving out, or casting out, a demon. The meaning of the Greek word for "cast out" is to expel, to force to go away, or to throw out. Louw-Nida uses the word exorcise to describe the practice of making the demon leave. Therefore exorcise is a word having to do with confrontational deliverance.

Notice in this passage that the function or assignment of the demon was to make the man mute. This man had the root spirit called "deaf and dumb" in the Bible. There are other functions these root spirits could be associated with, such as crying, dissociation, multiple personality disorder, blindness, mental illness, ear problems, suicide, foaming at the mouth, seizures/epilepsy, gnashing of teeth, sickness leading to prostration, or extreme weakness. To make my point, demons never work alone! The spirit "deaf and dumb" has many who work for him, including some that bring sickness and some that take strength from the body!

Luke goes on to say that some were amazed, and some even came against Jesus and spoke evil of the power of God. Some of the people there attributed Jesus' work to Beelzebub, which reveals that a fallen angel was blinding their minds to keep them from the truth. Anyone who drifts away from non-confrontational or confrontation deliverance has some fallen angel controlling their minds. How do we know this? Because these types of deliverance are scriptural. There are people who don't accept the power of God in its different manifestations; they don't like or accept deliverance. These people speak evil about the work of the Holy Spirit. These people unknowingly speak from the heart of fallen principalities or second heaven rulers over this fallen age that we live in. Jesus confirms this in verse 18; he makes the point that driving out demons reveals the two invisible kingdoms. Jesus also states and confirms that Satan, the chief prince of the fallen angels, has a kingdom. This kingdom is set up first with thrones, second with dominions, third with principalities, and fourth with powers. Thrones have the most exalted position, while the others descend in order. Paul the Apostle lays out this overall structure in Colossians 1:16.

FALLEN ANGELS SEEK TO CONTROL AND INFLUENCE THE DIRECTION OF ALL CENTURIES, AGES, AND ETERNITIES.

"For by Him, all things were created that are in heaven and that are on earth, visible and invisible, whether thrones or dominions or principalities or powers. All things were created through Him and for Him. And He is before all things, and in Him, all things consist." (NKJV).

In each of these levels of power, there are different rulers and sub-rulers throughout the world. In each of these levels of the Fallen, in these spheres of jurisdiction within the second heaven, each of the rulers or fallen angelic majesties have a created order. It is an actual number used as a ranking system! This order determines where Satan and his ruling counsel assigned these beings. I know there are nine different classes of fallen angels on the four levels (thrones, dominions, principalities, and powers). Here are some of the names for fallen beings from 13 different Bible translations: glorious ones, glorious beings, angelic beings or majesties, celestial beings, dignitaries, supernatural beings, or those in exalted positions.

The second heaven or heavenly realm is where fallen angels, in their order or ranking, engage in spiritual warfare for the minds of men. These fallen angels seek to control and influence the course of countries, the lifespan of countries, times, seasons, and the direction of all centuries, ages, and eternities. This is their function! Let me give you a scriptural example. In Acts 13, Sergius Paulus was governor over the providence, he often kept private sorcerers or diviners. One of these, named Bar-Jesus, was a magician, a false prophet who practiced black magic, a master of the arts of witchcraft, an interpreter of omens and a revealer of secret things of the occult. The occultist sought wisdom, revelation, and power from evil fallen angels. Revelation 2:24 talks about the deep things or secret powers of the fallen realms. Let us pick a name that most believers are familiar with in the second heaven: A fallen angel who is a principality.

So what is the definition of a principality? Principalities are "first ones, preeminent ones, leaders,"- it means beginning, chief in order, time, place or rank; old or ancient; author, captain, prince. Look closely at when they were created – before Adam at the beginning. Not only is this definition true, but it has been confirmed through countless personal power encounters. Also, notice that there are rankings like a captain or prince; Daniel even calls some kings. However, when we look at how the Bible defines the demonic, they are described as mere supernatural beings or evil spirits who are sent to bring harm, distress, and ruin. There is nothing concerning rulership when it comes to their order in the creation.

What does a person's spirit feel when accused and under the power of a fallen angel? They feel pressure from the neck up, headaches, dizziness, confusion, difficulty concentrating, and experience nausea similar to motion sickness. Governor Sergius Paulus was using this occultist Bar-Jesus to maintain power and control. But demons do not have that kind of power. Christian believers have been given authority over demons, but not necessarily over fallen angels from the second heaven. The second heaven only responds to, "it is written", in the courtroom of God.

THE GOAL IS TO ROB THEM OF THEIR INFLUENCE OVER THE HUMAN MIND, WILL, AND EMOTIONS BY TEARING THEM TO PIECES.

Now that the stage is set, Luke 11:20-23 talks about driving out demons by the finger of God or the power of God. Jesus said that if one of His disciples was driving out demons, then people would be witnessing the power of the kingdom of God. Don't be someone who slanders like evil spirits, or who becomes skeptical, or who has to test God. In verse 23, Jesus divides humanity into two groups, those who are with Him and those who are against Him. Deliverance is that tool that reveals man's allegiance.

Jesus says that no kingdom fighting against itself will stand. It will eventually fall. Those who doubt power encounters (the slanderers, and skeptics) contribute to an internal battle, one in which the army will destroy itself.

Just as armies in the natural realm have rankings, from privates to generals, so it is in the spiritual realm. These rankings are what I was talking about with the thrones, dominions, principalities, powers in the celestial realms, and demons in the terrestrial realms. The "finger of God" that Luke mentioned in verse 20 finds its origin in Exodus 8:19 when the occultist tried to duplicate the plague of gnats in Pharaoh's attempt to discredit the power of God. There is always something spiritually wrong when God's power is mocked. Notice how the occultist in Luke was brought to Jesus. Very few can come on their own because two opposing influences are at work: faith and unbelief.

Early in my healing and deliverance ministry, I had a woman come to the ministry for deliverance. We started to minister, taking her through inner- healing and then deliverance. About an hour into the ministry session, a demon came up and said, "You can't touch me, I am fully armed." Of course, we don't listen to demons, but at times they will brag and boast about what they have done or how they are armed. Anything that comes from evil spirits is deceptive, but it may be a partial truth. Satan misled Adam and Eve by using words that were deceptive and imperfect in truth. There was just enough truth to make Adam and Eve question the word of God. I have heard many threats and proclamations from evil spirits but I did not place any weight on this one's claim. However, its statement was true to a point. This strongman was fully armed, and I was untrained. Because of this, I was unable to help her any further in her quest for freedom.

Somehow this evil spirit knew that I did not have any experience with this kind of spiritual warfare, and did not have knowledge on how to approach this situation. He also must have had some knowledge of who I was, like in Acts 19:15, where that evil spirit knew about Paul. Evil spirits are aware of when we fighting back against spiritual warfare in their realm.

In this evil age, there are two kingdoms at work. The strongman here in scripture represents Satan, but on a smaller scale, it represents one of the chief spirits in charge. Remember, the kingdom of darkness is a highly structured and organized kingdom with descending orders of authorities, and different rulers and sub-rulers that are responsible for different areas of authority. There are always levels of authority within demonization or possession.

A strongman's house is his kingdom (his reign, rule, laws, power, and influences). It is what the strongman calls his property. He is also the main evil spirit that influences the sin, lawlessness, and transgression that bring about possession. It is the job of the strongman to build his kingdom within the mind, will, and emotions of an individual and their past generations. Most strongmen are generational, and so it could take many sessions to get to the chief strongman. Depending on the demonic structure within the person, a deliverance minister could run into many strongmen!

Notice what Jesus says about plunder. To plunder by definition is to attack in such a way that we gain control over the strongman's reign. The goal is to rob them of their influence over the human mind, will, and emotions by tearing them to pieces. We are to bring such hardship that we start seizing all their goods, booty, spoil, and possessions. What is under their possession? Emotional trauma, wounding, legal rights, the lawlessness that gives evil spirits entry for possession, and curses that bring iniquity into our bloodlines.

Why bind these strongmen? Bind means to tie up, to tie together, or to tie into bundles. Notice that this means binding not just one evil spirit, but all who work for that evil spirit. It means to tie evil spirits to their chief demon, and in this manner, the chief demon will speak for those tied to him. What is the purpose of binding? The purpose is to restrict, prohibit, imprison or to stop their work. Binding them together as biblical definition commands us to do, brings those demons to a central point, for judgment. To bind any evil spirit, we must overcome them by taking their legal rights, demolishing their strongholds, breaking their curses and generational curses, and by undoing witchcraft ceremonies and any rituals performed within that ceremony. We must think offensively! To overcome and defeat a combat platoon in the U.S. Marine Corp, you must get all of them or else they will be reassigned to another combat platoon.

To be fully armed is to be equipped with weapons and armor that are sufficient for battle. This is the true definition, and Jesus says these beings must be disarmed! Jesus says the only way to defeat a strongman is to take away their armor. That means it must be removed piece by piece! In order to remove the armor, you must understand what the armor of Satan consists of. Only through experience and training can you be successful at doing this!

The belt of lies is spiritual protection that hangs in front of the strongman's abdomen. It is a spiritual plate if you will that provides protection to the core of who the strongman is. It is the first piece of protective equipment the strongman puts on when his house comes under attack. The belt of lies clings closely and shields the most vulnerable areas of the fortress. The belt of lies shows itself as deceit (deception) and deceives with tongues of poison (dishonesty, slander, lies). This why it clings so closely. It is the first piece of armor that must come off because of the intense lies that are going through the mind of the individual seeking freedom.

The belt of lies readies the strongman for action. If the strongman can get the person to believe these lies, he will not be in jeopardy of being expelled, and he can defend most of his fortress. The belt of lies is always ready to defend against the power of truth and revelation knowledge. Its function is to talk you out of truth and lock down your mind. Mental issues can be formed from this piece of the armor.

The second piece of the Satanic armor is the breastplate of unrighteousness. The breastplate tells the person that they are an evildoer, sinful, unholy, impure, wicked, hard-hearted, crooked, perverse and that they surrender to evil impulses and engage in evil deeds. The breastplate focuses on the actions of sin the possessed person committed. Wrapped around the strongman's chest, these are curved spiritual transgressions with many bands of sin. Chains of sins are woven together until they form a vest or breastplate against the person. These unrighteous deeds must be forgiven and renounced.

IT IS POSSIBLE FOR DEMONIZATION TO HAVE BEEN WITH HUMANITY SINCE THE FALL.

The purpose of the breastplate of unrighteousness is to protect the strongman's vital organs. It is the strongman's job to assign infirmities to attack the organs of the demonized person.

The third piece of Satanic armor are the shoes of torment, suffering, pain, stress, worry, anxiety, fear, panic attack, sickness, disease, and infirmity. These are all things that go against the spirit of faith and truth. In the Bible, there are many verses that talk about walking by faith, not by sight (2 Cor.5:7). Since marching was an essential part of a soldier's life, his shoes were very important. The breaking of a soldier's shoe was a metaphor for weakness or defeat. It is the strongman who ultimately holds the weaknesses of the person.

In Ephesians 6:15, the Greek word for preparation or readiness can also be translated as a prepared foundation. In other words, a firm basis for a soldier's feet. Someone who has shoes of torment will continue to walk in falsehood and their lives will consist of one disaster after another. In this state, there will be no long-term peace, unity, or freedom.

The fourth piece of the Satanic armor is the shield of unbelief – rebellion (defiance), skepticism, atheism, doubt, unwillingness to acknowledge the truth, conceit, prideful reasoning, blinded through ignorance, disobedience, and other strongholds. Before going into battle, Roman soldiers drenched their leather covered shields with water. The shield stood four feet long and three feet wide, it was covered with calf or goat skin. These water-soaked skins immediately put the flames out of the fiery arrows of the enemy. The soldiers would put their shields together so that they would have more protection. These evil arrows meant testing, temptation, lies, distractions, all of which would bring unbelief and rebellion if they hit their target.

The helmet of condemnation is the fifth piece to the armor of Satan. It is designed to render a verdict of guilt often with punishment. This helmet brings torment in the mind through feelings of guilt, shame, inferiority, and dwelling on mistakes. This helmet is why many people experience headaches, confusion, forgetfulness, and nausea like motion sickness. Fallen angels seek to attach themselves to the mind! In the Roman world, this helmet was made out of iron or bronze, with two cheek pieces to protect the soldier's face. The helmet protected the skull and neck. The helmet of condemnation points to the strongman's victory over the person, holding their mind in some form of captivity.

The final piece of Satanic armor is the hammer of judgment. Its function is to pass judgment, be opinionated, plant false wisdom and discernment, and stir up dark secrets and motives of the heart that show disrespect, disapproval, and hatred. Have you ever been around someone who has heard the gospel and seen the work of the Holy Spirit, yet is always finding something wrong? This is a person who likes to judge people. They reason in their own mind what is right or wrong. It is from the realm of disrespect and jealousy. Disapproval reveals hatred in the deeper places. If someone wonders whether there is a strongman governing their life, take them to a church meeting where deliverance and exorcism are going on, and talk to them afterward to see what they say!

We all want to model the early church, at least I do. So if this is the case, we must realize that demonization and exorcism were not uncommon then and they won't be now. The New Testament testifies to the existence of Jewish exorcists other than Jesus and the apostles. Luke 11:19 in our text points out that the disciples of the Pharisees practiced exorcism and in Acts 19 seven sons of a Jewish priest named Sceva attempted to cast out demons in Jesus' name. Luke 9:49 speaks of a man outside the group of disciples who were casting out demons in Jesus' name. If demonization appeared in the Old Testament, like in the account of King Saul being tormented by an evil spirit, then it is possible for demonization to have been with humanity since the fall.

Remember Ephesians 6:12 says, "For our wrestling match is not against flesh and blood [contending only with physical opponents], not against persons with bodies, but against cosmic powers and or fallen angels who rule with various areas and descending orders of authority. Against world dominators of this present darkness, against spiritual forces of wickedness in the heavenlies" (AMP).

Chapter Five

Spiritual Warfare and Authority

Matthew 4:17 states that Jesus began to preach or to publicly announce kingdom truths and principles while urging acceptance and compliance to His message. He began teaching to impart skills and knowledge concerning the kingdom of God that would change the course of this evil age. It is the job of Bible teachers to participate in the supernatural in such a way that the Word of God imparts supernatural skills and methods that transform the way the Church is seen by the world. The Bible says, from that time, meaning a period of time forward indefinitely from that point. This beginning of Jesus' ministry would initiate a process, which, through a series of actions would establish a kingdom rule and government, that would be first in rank and power and would have power over all other rule.

The kingdom comes to believers when we first accept and obey the truths, principles and power of Jesus' reign. Jesus established a rule where He would be first in rank and He began to regulate the works of evil that are done under the sun through the Church, the body of Christ. To restrain evil, the cross must be preached, with a demonstration of power. The gospel is a message of truth, yes, but it is also a message of power. Jesus' teaching was twofold in manifestation: to destroy the works of Satan in this age and secondly, at the end of the age Jesus will destroy the Kingdom of Darkness. In this evil age the works of Satan, that is fallen angel and demonic spirits of all kinds, are destroyed by the binding of their legal rights to the sin, transgression, and iniquity of humanity. This is how evil is destroyed!

TO RESTRAIN EVIL, THE CROSS MUST BE PREACHED, WITH A DEMONSTRATION OF POWER.

The Church has been called to move in power that influences righteousness. This, in turn, looses mankind from evil and binds the powers of darkness from their work. Yet most Churches don't know the power and authority that it takes to transform regions from darkness to light, because they are untrained in spiritual warfare. It is the believer's lack of understanding of spiritual warfare that keeps regions bound in darkness. We know that the power of the Kingdom of God is righteousness, yet most don't see that the power of the Kingdom of darkness is sin.

Explaining the second aspect of Jesus' teaching, at the end of the age, Jesus will destroy the Kingdom of Darkness. We read about this in 1 John 3:8, Jesus was manifested that He might destroy the works of the devil. Again, the power of the devil or the Kingdom of Darkness is sin. We know from 1 Cor. 15:56 that sin is a power. If sin is a power, then we must conclude that sin is also a person and whose desire is to influence a course of action. When the Bible makes reference to Satan, a lot of the time, it is to the Kingdom of Darkness, sin, and a course or direction.

We see in Mark 1:24 (NASB) one demon speaking for those under his authority saying, what business do we have with each other. Business is related to a person's regular occupation, profession, or trade. It is an activity that someone is engaged in, involved in or concerned about. This is what demons do! Their business or tradecraft is to cause mankind to choose or purchase sin. Many times I have accused demons of making the person sin, but the demons always answer back, "Yes we influenced them, but they chose." Through that simple statement is a bigger picture. Their business is to influence mankind to follow the ways of sin and human desire which gives the rulers of this evil age power. The power of free will can set us free or bring us into captivity, but it is always a choice, Romans 6:16.

The demon asked Jesus if He had come to destroy us; this one demon speaking for many. Jesus came first to destroy their works and to drive the first of three nails in evil's coffin. Jesus' death on the cross has rendered the

THE POWER OF THE KINGDOM OF DARKNESS IS SIN.

kingdom of darkness powerless, and that powerlessness is extended through His Church as we institute atmospheres of righteousness and justice. That first nail broke the power of sin and gave mankind the ability to be freed from sin, transgression, and iniquity. The second nail is to come, the return of Christ Jesus at the millennium in which evil spirits, both in the celestial and terrestrial realms, will be imprisoned for a thousand years. The third and final nail is when all sin and powers have been placed under Jesus' feet and He hands the Kingdom of God over to the Father, this marks the beginning of the Age to Come, when the perfect reality of the Kingdom of God is ushered in.

I have heard some say, that scripture teaches that the beginning of the conflict with demons or the powers of darkness is in the courtroom. In my experience, however, I have seen that conflict with darkness is fought in righteousness through choices. In my experience and through scripture, I just cast out demons whenever I run into them. Yes, there are legal rights, curses, strongholds, witchcraft entanglement, oaths, vows etc... that must be broken, but like Jesus, He just cast them out after rebuking them for their wrongdoing. Rebuking in the Bible is to reprimand or chastise for wrong. It is an undoing of what evil spirits have the right too.

I do agree, there is a courtroom experience, however, there is also a battlefield experience. Yet these two positions have two completely different levels of spirit beings. A believer who is well trained, experienced in spiritual warfare through thousands of combat encounters knows which position to take, courtroom or battlefield. This believer also knows through many deliverances, in the celestial and terrestrial realm, that respecting the enemy is a key and godly principal.

Spiritual authority is such a big subject. Without proper training and practical experience, a lot of unnecessary information has been printed. Wisdom is the capacity to understand and as a result, to act wisely and in power. So to operate in authority, we must understand the rules of engagement in the realm we desire to operate in and to act wisely in exercising that power. Authority is the right to use power, but for power to have an effect or to succeed, it must be used correctly. This is why we must be fully trained. Someone who is properly trained in authority will exhibit signs of power.

Wisdom, understanding, proper training and the gifts of the Holy Spirit will give guidance, direction, and even warnings. Yet, too many believers say things like, the devil has no power, but go on minutes later and sin, in act or thought, not knowing that it is the devil's nature in them that is causing them to sin, looking for legal rights to enter them. This is not wisdom! Wisdom says, I recognize that a power and person is tempting me, looking to enter my life and possess me, so I resist the temptation and it will flee.

Through many unusual supernatural encounters, whether by voice, leading or unction, scripture, or manifestation in spiritual warfare, God has continued to change and develop me in spiritual warfare. I have seen too many

Christians experience heartbreaking tragedies like divorce, family issues, sexual immorality, drugs, even sickness due to incorrect spiritual warfare techniques and the wrong use of authority. Never fail to comprehend the enemies authority and their right to use their authority to influence mankind.

In Luke 10:17-20, we see the seventy (two) disciples return with joy saying, Lord, even the demons are subject to us in Your name. I have always found an inner joy in casting out demons. In my early days, I would even call my friends and express my joy to them. This should be a supernatural experience for the believer who casts out evil spirits. Joy is one of the fruit for those who experience deliverance. When there's no joy, deliverance has taken place, but much is still to be accomplished in that person.

What does it mean that evil spirits are subject to believers in Jesus name? It means to submit to the orders or directives of someone and to be brought under control of Christ. Let me say this a little more clearly! The believer is to bring the evil spirits engaged under the dominion and control of Christ Jesus' Kingdom through spiritual warfare principals, orders or directives, forcefully making the spirits obey. Dominion or control is the understanding of authority that is necessary to exercise power over that sphere of operation to bring change. There are many spheres of

TOO MANY BELIEVERS SAY THINGS LIKE, THE DEVIL HAS NO POWER, BUT GO ON MINUTES LATER AND SIN.

operation in the demonic realm, as there are also many spheres of operation in the fallen angel realm, and in each, they overlap in some measure. What the believer is doing, is bringing a sphere, level or dimension of authority and power over those evil spirits within that level of evil. To boil it all down, authority is given to the believer, but to see the power of that authority, that comes through training. We see this in the Bible, where the disciples spent three years with Jesus and then continued their training under the Holy Spirit.

Jesus said He was watching Satan's kingdom falling or He was a spectator while looking at the disciples enforcing God's rule by casting out demons. Whenever the Church starts moving in power through spiritual warfare, Satan's kingdom, whether personally or geographically begins to fall. Jesus used the term, lightning, for the fall of the devil's kingdom, and it means with suddenness. What causes lightning? When a cloud with a negatively charged bottom and a positively charged top is separated by an atmosphere, acting as an insulator, which can no longer keep these two electrical fields apart. This is spiritual warfare! When the children of God no longer decide that an atmosphere should separate the two kingdoms, then lightning, power and authority, is exercised which causes the kingdom of darkness to fall. That intermediate atmosphere is often the lack of desire to be trained properly and learn correctly how to exercise power and authority in spiritual warfare.

DEMONS ARE EVIL SPIRITS WHO WORK UNDER THE AUTHORITY AND CONTROL OF FALLEN ANGELS.

Thunder is caused by lightning. When a lightning bolt travels from the cloud to the ground it actually opens up a little hole in the air, called a channel. Once the bolt of electrically charged ions has passed through the channel, the air collapses back and creates a sound wave that we hear as thunder. As evil spirits are being expelled, a spiritual channel is opened and a sound wave in the spirit realm is made. Jesus heard in the spirit realm these evil spirits being sent to the pit or the abyss. We also hear it in the physical realm, we just don't understand what we hear. The Bible calls it screaming or to cry out! This crying out is when the realm of the dead opens as the evil spirits are cast out of the person and sent to the pit.

Jesus also meant, while you were expelling the subordinates, the demons, I was seeing their master Satan fall. Pathways are opened and spiritual sounds are made in the spirit realm as the children of God engage in spiritual warfare to bring down the Kingdom of Darkness. This is why other evil spirits come from different areas or spiritual dimensions and rally around or as the definitions explain, come to the aid of those being judged. Let me explain, we see this in Mark 1, the first cry in verse 23 is the spirit speaking through the man, the second cry, in verse 26, we see that same spirit now crying out for help because he is under judgement. As I've stated before, this is why we are to make evil spirits submit to the orders or directives and to be brought under the dominion and control unto obedience to Christ. It is as important to understand spiritually what is taking place as it is to properly engage in spiritual warfare.

This brings us to a point where we see in Luke 10 a hierarchy or a system of organization in which demons and fallen angels are grouped and are ranked according to status and authority. If we don't know how they are grouped and ranked, effective spiritual warfare cannot take place. This system is arranged by creative order, classification of beings according to their power, importance, and position in a sphere or territory, from first to last. We see this in Jude 6 where angels did not keep their own domain or sphere of authority in which one exercises a controlling influence. They abandoned or willfully gave up their claim to the Kingdom of God or their abode for their own will and the result was evil. This is why they call themselves fallen, named after this fallen evil age. Fallen angels have their spheres of authority as well as demons. They have spheres and consider these positions their own property. This is why evil spirits work so hard to set up strongholds.

THERE SHOULD BE AS MANY DELIVERANCES GOING ON AS HEALINGS IN MEETINGS.

Again in Luke 10, we see their property or sphere invaded by the disciples exercising proper spiritual authority with power to bring down demons, subordinates who are lower in rank, position, and in creation within that realm. Demons are evil spirits who work under the authority and control of fallen angels in territories, and within the organization of those territories according to hierarchical positions. What Jesus pictures and explains to His disciples is a very highly structured and well-organized kingdom with descending orders of authorities and different rulers and sub-rulers responsible for different areas of authority, both in the earth and in the second heaven. This is why spiritual authority comes with knowledge and training through Biblical principles and practical experience as we take on the forces of darkness as the disciples did in Jesus' name under His instruction. The Bible has some wonderful guidelines and even secrets for spiritual warfare, and it is for those who participate in wisdom and discover those truths. As stated earlier, wisdom is the capacity to understand and as a result, to act wisely and in power.

Spiritual warfare is about authority, but healing is about power. This is why Jesus has given the Church power and authority to heal the sick and to cast out demons. I have ministered both corporately and privately, to a lot of believers who have been under many powerful healing ministries, yet have been possessed with evil spirits. We fail as the body of Christ when we focus on only healing and not deliverance. There should be as many deliverances going on as healings in meetings. We also fail when we don't recognize that there are spirit beings that have places of influence over regions, territories, institutions, family bloodlines, and individuals both in the demonic realm and in the second heaven or fallen angelic realm. These spirits seek to control atmospheres, cultures, human activity, and different ways of life through possession.

The purpose of the Church is to engage these spiritual strongholds correctly and subdue their authority and power gained through different levels of sin. Levels of sin come through human actions, culture, civil laws, money and beliefs.

By pursuing spiritual warfare, we are freeing mankind in the terrestrial realm and the celestial realm. Authority understands that mankind must be freed bodily, mentally (soul) and spiritually. Spiritual authority also realizes that each realm must be dealt with according to the rules. There is no blanket prayer, declaration, renunciation, confession, or courtroom experience that brings total freedom without removing all the legal rights, according to how they are acquired, that can go as far back as Adam and Eve, which most do. This truth is positively identified as we engage with higher level evil spirits. The sins of the forefathers must be uncovered!

The Church should know that the different levels of the unseen realm control or influence the seen realm. When the Bible speaks of the heavens being shut up like bronze, it speaks about fallen angels who have control and influence over the minds of men and have legal rights and strongholds according to the decisions of man. These second heaven fallen angels have molded, shaped, and charmed mankind into the course and direction of this fallen age. This age is the age of sin, which leads to demonic possession and to come under fallen angel influence of the mind. Parts of our body and mind are controlled by evil.

Possession is of the body, where oppression is of the mind. Two completely different realms and two completely different spirit beings. The Church likes to draw a line of difference in this subject, this too proves that even within the Church minds are under fallen angel influence or control.

Possession is defined in the Bible as to exercise and influence both the souls and bodies of men. We cannot reduce this definition to only demons. We must understand when a demon enters a man it is through choice, which is willful sin. The person has followed or acted in the way of the course of this evil age. Willfully choosing, like Adam and Eve, bringing mankind under the satanic nature and control. The influencing fallen angel in that territory assigns demons to work internally in mankind to complete the overall purposes and desires of this evil age. Territorial Spirits, with the sub-rulers, all the way down to individual demons work territorially in different areas to complete the purpose of this evil age. The overall purpose of this evil age is to cause mankind to renounce God, however, the way that happens in each area is different. The strategy of the evil age is going to be different in each city because the culture and influence of the church is different everywhere.

This is another key, deliverance is not a one-time event. This is understanding spiritual warfare and operating in authority and power correctly. Spiritual warfare has become a ministry and has become focused on a case by case basis and that is the problem. Spiritual warfare should be seen geographically first. It should be studied individually with the understanding of territorial freedom.

When we study the life of Christ, from His baptism and the Holy Spirit coming upon Him to His resurrection, his life was characterized by spiritual warfare. As Jesus taught, healed, and delivered, the kingdom of Satan resisted in every way. We see the more the kingdom of God was displayed in power, the more darkness fought to blind the minds of men. So, Jesus has now left us with a commission, making disciples of all nations, teaching them to do what Jesus did, and we should know, that resistance is warfare.

AS JESUS TAUGHT, HEALED, AND DELIVERED, THE KINGDOM OF SATAN RESISTED IN EVERY WAY.

Revelation 3:8-10 teaches us that the Church today is to keep Jesus' word, not to deny His name or power, and we are to keep His command to persevere. Yes, we are to push through every trial and tribulation. We are to preach with demonstrations of power and witness in the name of Jesus, and we are to do what the word of God teaches, this too is spiritual warfare. Let me close this chapter out by saying, every demonic deliverance is an uncovering or revealing of fallen angels in families, bloodlines, organizations, territories and nations. For example, the more exorcisms an individual goes through, the more the stronghold of the chief demon in the body is revealed. When this starts to happen, fallen angels are unveiled and exposed so that the true bondage of the family becomes unwrapped. Remember, as demons run in groups, so do fallen angels in the second heaven.

Chapter Six

Overview of Healing

I am totally amazed that most of the Church is clueless to a world system that has no answers for the increasing problems of mankind. Even the Church itself seeks solutions outside of Christ Jesus. Any means of solving a problem or dealing with a difficult situation outside of biblical principle is only temporary. The world needs to see the Church proclaiming the message of Christ and see that message demonstrated in the supernatural. Yet most of the Church stays away from the healing message. Those who do embrace the message of healing only except it in parts. My goal for this chapter is to present an overall case for the message of healing. So let us start at the beginning and uncover the healing ministry as the Bible explains it.

For through the grace given to me, I say to every-one among you not to think more highly of him-self than he ought to think; but to think so as to have sound judgment, as God has allotted to each a measure of faith (Romans 12:3 NASB)

IF I DON'T EXERCISE SPIRITUAL GIFTS, THEY DO NOT GROW AND CANNOT BE SHARED.

The Apostle Paul tells us that each of us has been given a measure of faith. The word allotted here means, to deal out or to give out as one's portion or share. The word 'allotted' is the same Greek word used in Romans 1:11 for 'impart' which says, "For I long to see you so that I may impart some spiritual gift to you, that you may be established." That word 'impart' is so important to where we will be journeying in the realm of healing. We have discovered that each person has been given or dealt out, from God, a measure of faith. We also have uncovered that truth is dealt out through spiritual gifts. Gifts of the Holy Spirit taught through scriptural truth; faith can come to those who desire it. Let me say it this way! God has allotted faith, and Paul hungers to impart faith to grow and establish the Church. This same word 'allotted' is also translated in Ephesians 4:28 as "to share with." Paul the Apostle says, each person has been given a measure of faith. Faith also must be imparted, and faith must be shared. Sharing is doing! If I don't exercise spiritual gifts, they do not grow and cannot be shared.

Returning to our original scripture in Romans 12, let us talk about the word, measure. Measure means a unit of measurement, either of length or volume. Think of it this way, a twelve-ounce bottle will only hold twelve ounces. I need to fill up that bottle, and if I want more than twelve ounces, I need a bigger bottle. Faith is meant to grow, and as I share with those in need, I become established. It means that I am laying a firm foundation through faith so that the gift of healing can grow. There becomes an attitude of determination of acquiring of that which has been promised in scripture. So I continue to fill up and pour out my bottle until it's time to get a bigger bottle. As I exercise the healing gift, it will start to grow through faith.

The Apostle is talking about a faith that is not restricted to a justifying faith, but a faith as a condition of power. Most believers have not looked at faith as the avenue of power. Believers have heard it preached but seeking after it requires training. The condition of power elevates to offices, spiritual insights, functions, and abilities. It is impossible to please God or be promoted without exercising faith through power. Just because someone holds a Church office or is teaching a home fellowship, doesn't mean they have spiritual power. With faith the believer receives the power of discernment as to the actual limitations of his or her gifts, and the ability to grow the gift. Without training and the impartation or sharing of the knowledge, the believer is restricted or limited in exercising faith with power. This is why we don't see more healings in the Church today! Let me give you an example of what I'm saying! Smith Wigglesworth stated in one of his books, that the only way to deal with cancer is to treat it as a demonic issue. In healing and deliverance I have found that statement to be true.

After attending our church's supernatural class one of the young men went to pray for his grandmother that was lying on her deathbed. She was sent home through hospice to die. She was weak in body and could not turn over in bed by herself. He went over to her house and commanded the infirmity of cancer to come out of his grandmother. As the infirmity was coming out, he had to turn her on her side as she was vomiting a dark blackish green liquid. Within minutes the grandmother sat up all by herself, declared that Jesus had done a miracle, and her grandson had prayed with power. How did this all happen? I shared secrets of my history with God and imparted spiritual truth according to scripture in supernatural class. Without this impartation of truth and his belief, his grandmother would have died. She was so full of cancer that the doctors said there was nothing they could do for her. Seeking answers outside of Christ Jesus is only temporary. That demon of cancer will never touch her body again; glory to God!

IT IS IMPOSSIBLE TO PLEASE GOD OR BE PROMOTED WITHOUT EXERCISING FAITH THROUGH POWER.

Paul never says, the measure, but a measure. If it was the measure, it could not be added to or subtracted from. So a measure indicates that there can be more measures to be received.

Paul even takes this impartation further, by stating that he not only shared the gospel of power with the Thessalonians but his own life as well. I lead a power evangelism group from the supernatural class. We go out into the community and expect Jesus, through the Holy Spirit, to do signs and wonders. People are healed, delivered, and prophesied to, leading to salvation. It is amazing the human need out there!

Paul says it's not enough to teach you how to grow your faith based only on what God deposited, therefore, I must share with you the life of signs and wonders. Come out on the streets with and let's demonstrate that Christ Jesus is the same yesterday, today, and forever!

What is the basic principle of healing? It is this; if you can believe, nothing is impossible with God. The problem is getting people to believe. It's deeper than that. It is getting people to invest their time and be taught in healing. Scriptural knowledge, logic, and even medicine can get in the way. People seem to put more faith in those areas than in scripture and the power of the Holy Spirit.

SEEKING ANSWERS OUTSIDE OF CHRIST JESUS IS ONLY TEMPORARY.

Healing is not by random chance or selection but through a divine method. God does not have a healing lottery, but a divine method. He is not orderless in thought or behavior, but God has a systematic plan of healing. Derek Prince said in one of his books, if someone is not getting healed, then the conditions have not been met. We see this in Exodus.

> *And He said, "If you will give earnest heed to the voice of the Lord your God, and do what is right in His sight, and give ear to His commandments, and keep all His statutes, I will put none of the diseases on you which I have put on the Egyptians; for I, the Lord, am your healer." (Exodus 15:26 NASB)*

Notice there was and still are conditions! Sickness has its origin in sin. This is the foundational truth of healing. Some may ask, "I've lived a Christian lifestyle all my life, why am I sick?" My response is that there must be a curse in your family's bloodline. Yet some believers are not willing to accept this. They have the blanket belief that every curse hung on the cross with Jesus. This is true positionally in Christ. Conditionally, the curse still lives in the old man. Until Christ comes back, we are stuck with two natures. The new nature comes through being born-again. The old nature is continually dying or being put off.

Now, we can become sick due to our diets. Eating correctly after you've been healed is so important. To revisit the gluttony of sugar and carbohydrates can open the door to allow sickness to come back.

Faith is not necessarily free from doubt, but it is the presence of belief. Let me say it this way, whenever there is faith, doubt tries to creep in. The more we exercise faith, the more confident we become, and the less we doubt! Faith is not a feeling! We may not always feel like we have great faith, but because of history with God, it feels more like something normal. Let me say it this way, faith has become a part of you. As faith grows, there is an increase of spiritual power, and living by faith becomes normal Christianity.

People make the mistake of examining their faith. This is a fatal task. What they are doing is interrogating themselves. We were not called to analyze faith, but to exercise it. We are called to do what the Bible says concerning healing. That is to operate in faith.

In Mark 9:23, the Bible says that "all things are possible to him who believes." So many people teach this passage of scripture in Mark 9:14-29 wrong. The first failure is that most are unsuccessful in seeing all the demonic activity in the passage. There are many demons in operation. Second, most teach that the disciples did not have enough faith to cast them out. Yet James says, faith without works is dead. The disciples were exercising the faith they knew by trying, but could not get it out. This is so simply explained. Some will even call to Matthew 17:20, this too is simply explained. Littleness is defined in Matthew 17 as to not have enough faith or to have limited faith. It means a state of having little or inadequate faith. The disciples ran into something they had never experienced before. A different level of evil. They lacked training! Their method was unsuccessful.

When we experience something new in the spirit realm, it is seen naturally as a lack of faith. The truth is we lack understanding, and so we cannot exercise spiritual truth which operates from faith. But it was promotion day for the disciples! Lack of results when exercising your training means that promotion has come upon you. You are now in a realm of the supernatural that is new and must be investigated. It is an invitation to the more! This has happened to me at least five times. What looks like a defeat that day was nothing more than spiritual promotion. For example, in the chapter of this book I shared about a strongman fully armed. That day, I ran into an evil spirit that I've never had training for, so I could not get the armed strongman out. I had never encountered an armed strongman. His armor protected him from my spiritual warfare training. Jesus was promoting me. It looked like a failure at the time. But through study, I found out that the Satanic armor was real, and I need to disarm his armor. So now, when I run into the strongman, since I've experienced it, through spiritual warfare, now I'm trained. I am now trained to disarm and expel the strongman. The same thing happens in the healing ministry. The more we embrace healing, the more we grow, and the more ability we have to bring healing and breakthrough to people.

Another thing we must understand in healing, time issues are not the characteristic mark of healings and miracles. I've had people touched by the power of God, yet show no physical signs of being healed. Later, when I hear from them or see them, they are healed. The power or touch from God is the healing seed deposited. When this happens we are to grow that seed. Then healing starts to take place.

WHAT LOOKS LIKE A DEFEAT THAT DAY WAS NOTHING MORE THAN SPIRITUAL PROMOTION.

There is a Greek word 'Sozo', which means to rescue or to deliver, the sense of averting some danger threatening life. It can be used as deliverance from war, danger in the sea, or deliverance from an illness. 'Sozo' when used as 'delivered from', means to have something removed from you. So healing is the removal of something. There are fourteen related passages of scripture talking about delivered from disease or demon possession. Let me list them: (Matt. 9:21, 22; Mark 3:4; 5:23, 28, 34; 6:56; 10:52; Luke 6:9; 8:36, 48, 50; 17:19; 18:42; John 11:12).

Let us look at a power encounter that involved the word 'Sozo' Mark 5:28 (AMP):

> *For she thought, "If I just touch His clothing, I will get well."*

Remember we said when 'Sozo' is used, as delivered from, it means to have something removed from you. This woman was in the crowd with a hemorrhage and had suffered extreme physical and emotional pain. In situations like this, I first consider deliverance from a spirit of infirmity. Joseph Thayer and Strong's definitions use 'Sozo' as to save a suffering one from disease that perishes or brings death. It is Greek number 4982 and is also used in a way that could include spiritual healing. She had gone to many physicians, but they were unable to help her. The condition continued to grow worse. This is a sign of an evil spirit of infirmity at work. In most cases, when someone is suffering, the root cause is sin that has led to infirmity possession. Doctor's cut out parts of our bodies, but the evil spirit is still there and continues to work. When she felt the power run through her body, she said, that she had been freed from her suffering. She felt the power of God and the infirmity left her.

Like so many, when prayed for, people say that they felt something leave their body. They even at times expel wind in many forms. People also say that the pain is gone! According to scripture, this woman was freed from any charge of errors or sins that brought possession. When she was freed from those charges, her healing took place. People also say that they feel a vacant or empty place. That spirit of infirmity giving life to the disease left, and so they feel empty. Yes, giving life to diseases, these are spirits of infirmity. An example is cancer; a spirit of infirmity gives life to cancer. Cancer has a function, but it is the evil spirit's job to give it life. Once the spirit leaves, the disease dies. This is a proven method! Hundreds have gone through this process with cancer. Other long-term diseases must be handled in this matter. Again, it is the biblical pattern or method of healing.

When people are healed through power ministry; evil spirits are driven out by power. The spiritual conditions to their healing have been met, and the infirmity leaves. Some are so clueless about this revelation. The reason is that they have not spent twenty years casting out demons and being educated on how evil works. If the sickness returns, the spiritual conditions were not met, and the evil infirmity returns to its house. It is just that simple.

One more thing about healing here before we move on. Sickness can return if we don't eat healthily. I remember a woman who was delivered of sugar diabetes, and within five days her insulin levels returned to normal. She had a spirit of infirmity called sugar diabetes which affected the body's ability to produce insulin in the pancreas. When that evil infirmity came out, she felt pain in the pancreas as the spirit left, and was healed. But because of unchanged eating habits, the spirit returned. We are called to the stewardship of our bodies, not gluttony!

In the gospel of Luke, we see ten men who had leprosy. They met Jesus as He was traveling to a village between Samaria and Galilee. This too has the same meaning! When leprosy left him, he was made well or restored to health. Once the spirit leaves, then I'm instructed to pray for divine healing. One of two things will happen! The person can recover over a period of time or they will be made whole or healed instantaneously. The disciples were very well trained from the beginning, instructed by Jesus to cast out demons and then to heal the sick. Today we have those who do one or the other, not me! I do both!

So what is the difference between miracles and healing? Miracles are the creation of something, the renewal of something. They add to what you had or restore or regenerate what you had. Healings are when something is removed. A miracle follows healing according to scripture. How else could something be added or fixed if the broken is not first removed?

Chapter Seven

The Error of Slandering the Fallen

Throughout Church history, God has used scripture, prophetic words, dreams, and supernatural encounters to give guidance, direction, training, and even warnings. Those who understood the message, who obeyed, were delivered from all kinds of evil.

Most Christian believers think they have spiritual authority when they really do not. For most Christians, they lack the knowledge to move in authority. For example, if I go and buy a house and get a loan from a bank, the bank owns the house until I pay them off. Spiritual warfare is no different. I must make an effort and take the time to experience the training process and undergo spiritual warfare combat situations. Without combat situations, I only think I'm ready. The classroom is important, but live-fire makes the warrior.

When we attack principalities and powers, called fallen angels, over geographical territories, family bloodlines, and organizations, we open ourselves up to an onslaught of destructive power. To not respect who they are in the creation and the power that they have through the sinful nature or satanic nature, is a big mistake. This is what it means to slander. Again, I use words like satanic nature, as a way of expressing mankind's physical body and mind under the control of Satan and the fallen angels through sin. This is why our minds must be renewed and why we must be delivered from evil. What believer's fail to see and comprehend is that those fallen angels have the authority and the right to retaliate according to scripture if we step outside the lines of scripture.

MOST CHRISTIAN BELIEVERS THINK THEY HAVE SPIRITUAL AUTHORITY WHEN THEY REALLY DO NOT.

The work of fallen angels is to twist and distort through perverted mindsets, calling good, evil and evil, good. We must understand that God allows Satan and the fallen angels to exist and operate in this fallen age. We also must understand that God has dominion over all His creation. God also retains the right to judge the fallen angels or the heavenly realms. I want to say it this way, God is the one who decides when the Fallen are judged. Yet, in the terrestrial realm, God has given mankind the right and authority to exercise dominion over demonic spirits. We don't pray them out, we cast them out!

Those that write or speak about demonic principalities reveal their lack of understanding of the realm, and we should quickly discard their findings and writings. The rights of demonic spirits are completely different than the rights of fallen angels.

WE MUST UNDERSTAND THAT GOD ALLOWS SATAN AND THE FALLEN ANGELS TO EXIST AND OPERATE IN THIS FALLEN AGE.

The Bible in Job 41 uses Leviathan as a metaphor for the fallen angels and Satan himself. Because of the fall of mankind, the believer's sinful nature has placed them under the power of the fallen angels through sin. Our born again spirit through Christ Jesus has placed us over the fallen angels. To defeat the Fallen, we must stand and operate according to our position in Christ. We are accused by the fallen angels according to the satanic nature, that is the fallen nature. This is where the battle is, the battle over the dual natures. So as long as we live in the flesh, this evil age, the satanic nature or principal, we are a little lower than the angels, good or evil. Remember, an angel is an angel even if those angels fell through sin. Just as we fell through sin, we did not become something else, we are still human.

The Bible teaches that even Satan and the Fallen wrongly used authority God had given them. This led to their fall through disobedience, rebellion and judgment, and at the close of the age they will be eternally punished. Those that believe they can bind fallen angels over families, churches, geographical regions, or nations operate in presumption, some idea or personal view that they think is true. This idea comes from a revelation falsely perceived and discerned. It is a vain imagination which only offers false hope. This is what God is telling Job. Let me give an example! If a family wants to be delivered from a fallen angel, the whole family must choose, and come together to be delivered. The same is true in regions. The people of those regions must come together and choose. The mistake that untrained writers and preachers make is that the Fallen looks at mankind as a whole. The Fallen's power is the sin and laws that mankind choose to live under. These laws are outside of God's law. Even Paul suggested to the Corinthians that there should be no divisions among the believers in the church. That they would be perfectly united in mind and thought. This is a warning to churches that fallen angels have the right to oppress churches and individuals through divisions. Here is something else I have seen, healings and miracles can be taking place in a church, yet believers are possessed with demons and under the control of fallen angels. This takes us back to the dual natures.

To the soldier, that is the believer, who has not spent years in combat, the enemy lays traps by giving small victories, to lead them and through them, many astray. The design of the Fallen is to bring harm to the body of Christ, not so much the individual.

Believers in Christ have these statements like, "I come against" or "I bind or I break off." They are directly coming against the principalities in that area and through some false imagination of spiritual power are slandering fallen angels. They want to wrestle with Fallen principalities without sufficient instruction and training and the result is absolutely no change to that region. They are being set up for destruction, sickness or even death. The person who engages in true spiritual warfare knows that attempting to bind territorial fallen angels over cities is as Solomon says, vanity of vanities. We can free those who desire that level of freedom.

THE DESIGN OF THE FALLEN IS TO BRING HARM TO THE BODY OF CHRIST, NOT SO MUCH THE INDIVIDUAL.

If we want to break the power of fallen angels in the second heaven over regions, we pray, proclaim the gospel, and demonstrate or if I can say, use the power of the Holy Spirit. Salvation is only the beginning. Then believers must submit to deliverance or even exorcism, both in the terrestrial and celestial realms, on all levels. To even imagine that someone could repent, go through curse breaking, renounce soul ties, renounce strongholds or go to the court of heaven without multiple exorcisms, is like chasing after the wind. It sounds 'spiritual', but so do half-truths!

The evidence is in the change of families, churches, cities, regions, and nations. Just a word of advice, if we don't have great understanding and power over demons, what makes us think the fathers or sires of the demons will obey. Stop and repent for unscriptural behavior in coming against and falsely trying to bind fallen angels. Repent for trying to take authority over the principality, his region, through any falsely perceived spiritual power. Anyone who has wisdom and revelation in the realms of fallen angels realizes that it is God who judges in the heavenly realms.

Some of the major hampers that stop the Kingdom of God from being manifested are mindsets and beliefs. Resistance from the kingdom of darkness comes on many levels. There are thrones and sub-thrones, dominions and sub-dominions, principalities and sub-principalities, and last or lowest in the second heaven is powers, with sub-powers. This leads many believers into some false reality of spiritual warfare. It is as if they must say or do something like binding or loosing.

Here is one for you, why would anyone have to go to the court of heaven and ask God for a judgment over a demonic spirit? The Bible is so clear, cast or drive out demonic spirits on all terrestrial levels.

Let me say, we have had amazing breakthroughs in spiritual warfare. There has been incredible fruit universally in the body of Christ, but we still lack the secrets to the kingdom of darkness. Remember, don't let some form of success convince us that it has been endorsed or warranted by God. I find most of the time when someone has chosen the wrong method but gets breakthrough, they have already asked God, and the conditions have already been met.

To think we can go to the courts of heaven and obtain a judgment from God when repentance by individuals, churches, organizations, cities, regions or nations has not been made, is slanderous in nature. To think that we could agree with the court of heaven and that would silence a fallen angel, is presumption. This proves someone has taken an idea or action to be true and it started a chain of other ideas or arguments. This is deception! In court, both sides have their arguments, it is who can prove their case!

Slander in the heavenly realms is to misunderstand or have the wisdom and knowledge but act unscripturally. It is more than just saying something, it is a mindset or belief. It can even be like writing a book with false direction through human reason or believing a single situation that results in a breakthrough. The enemy will give small victories, so that deception may rule.

So, when we act more out of wisdom, demonstrating righteousness, doing the things the gospel commands, God then removes certain fallen angels in the second heaven. Other fallen angels must be removed through a direct confrontation in prayer and fasting. God simply sends them down, and as they accuse us of our guilty satanic nature, we repent and rebut from our scriptural position in Christ Jesus. Whether it is spiritual warfare or understanding who we are in Christ, it all comes down to our position over our condition. We must exercise our position over our condition.

The law condemns our sinful condition, that is the old man who is with us unto death, because we were born under the power of sin. Only death will separate us from this body and power of sin. Here will be a truth that might be hard to swallow, through the carnal nature, the devil and fallen angels have rights to humanity. To think otherwise is to be deceived. This was revealed many years ago in a second heaven encounter with the devil himself. As I prayed and he accused and debated over biblical scripture, I realized that through the carnal nature the devil had access. This was also Jesus' desert experience; we cannot mishandle scripture and sin by doing it.

Our position in Christ Jesus is His nature living through our spirit. This born-again spirit-filled man is free in Christ, yet there is another principal working in my members, resisting my spirit man, until my departure of this fallen evil age in which I was naturally born into. So, when we increase in revelation, wisdom and righteousness through actions, the evil governing powers in our area are brought down for judgment. When these powers are forbidden to resist ministries, God's blessings come upon mankind. God has called His people to wisdom and discernment through actions as we go through spiritual warfare.

JESUS DID NOT SLANDER NOR DISRESPECT THE DEVIL THROUGHOUT THE TEMPTATIONS AND TRIALS.

Spiritual warfare on any level exposes the believer and the church to the enemy. The Fallen, with their demonic army, knows who we are and the level of training that we operate in. This was demonstrated when a minister I know went to Waco, Texas to free God's people from 3 ruling fallen angels over that territory. This minister only lasted 4 years in that territory before being driven out by those fallen angels. What happened?

The mindsets of those believers could not believe the work of the Holy Spirit. Believers in Waco could not understand that it is the Holy Spirit who drives out evil. They could not accept personal exorcism, zip code exorcism or county exorcism. They were ok with the outpouring of the Holy Spirit and healing, but to deal with the enemy was unacceptable. The Fallen blinded the mind of the believers in Waco, and the ministry dried up.

FOR THOSE THAT SAY THE DEVIL HAS NO POWER OVER THEM, IS TO COME AGAINST OR SLANDER GOD'S WORD.

Paul was given many great revelations to destroy the works of the enemy, but that also exposed him to the enemy, and the minds of mankind controlled by the fallen angels. If we look hard enough, we can see those who have both free and captive minds by their beliefs and actions.

Through the mindsets of mankind, we knowingly or unknowingly, agree or disagree with the fallen angels. Eventually, we will speak our minds. By definition, reviling involves verbal abuse, railing, or scolding. In the book of Jude it says if we make derogatory remarks or accuse angels, good or bad, we have spoken against scripture.

Obedience and humility is the standard of God's Kingdom. Disrespect is not the way of God. We see that Jesus had His temptation in the desert; He spoke scripture in a face to face encounter. Jesus did not slander nor disrespect the devil throughout the temptations and trials. This was a courtroom trial, and because it was in the desert, maybe it was in the Devil's court, but for sure the Devil's realm.

One thing I have learned in second heaven spiritual warfare, fallen angels possess amazing intellect and incredible authority to exercise power. Fallen angels carry the false anointing or a supernatural presence that feels evil. They have gifts that can operate through the elements of the earth. God gave these gifts when He created them. Even though they fell, their gifts like ours when we fall, are irrevocable. When Satan fell, he took with him one-third of all the classes of angels. It appears through spiritual warfare that higher classes of angels influenced lower classes of angels to rebel, choosing, like us, through their free will. We know from Jude 6 that these fallen angels had designated positions of power, and chose to leave those realms. Satan's kingdom operates no longer in the third heaven but is structured according to the Fallen's previous positions of authority. This is not an unproven revelation or assumption but is demonstrated by spiritual warfare encounters. The fallen angels have powers, and this determines their authority on the earth from the second heaven. We must be very careful how we speak to them, by non-direct or direct words.

For those that say the devil has no power over them, is to come against God's Word, to slander. God would not have revoked the Fallen's gifting; violating His own law. Peter tells us that some are not afraid to speak evil of dignitaries or majesties, knowing that angels are greater in power and might.

We know that Satan and the angels who followed him fell from their original created positions. We know that Jesus defeated him and his kind, yet he and the fallen angels still retain the dignity of their former positions until the end of the age. Believers in Christ Jesus have been called to demonstrate the multifaceted wisdom of God, and to reveal God's countless aspects of might, to the angelic rulers and authorities in the heavenly places, both good and bad. The Church is also to follow Jesus' pattern of ministry over the Fallen, which is above every name that has rule or authority, both in this age and the age to come. The Church is to enter this conflict, not so much as one individual but as a body. This too is a principle I've learned while encountering high-level second heaven fallen angels.

Chapter Eight

Overview of Territorial Spirits

We will start off this chapter by looking at one scripture that has overall guidelines for spiritual warfare and prayer.

The heavens are the heavens of the Lord, But the earth He has given to the sons of men. (Psalm 115:16 NASB)

We quickly see that mankind cannot pretend or make some assumed declaration that reaches into the heavenly realms or the celestial realms. We, in ourselves or in Christ, have no authority to rebuke Satan or the fallen angels since they are in the heavens. The proper response, the Lord rebuke you, like Michael the archangel as in Jude 9. We make these false presumptions and use them to base or adopt a particular attitude or feeling. We make these outlandish statements that have no visible power. This is unacceptable and arrogant behavior. Transgressing the limits of what is permitted by God's law, as in Psalm 115:16. We see that the heavens are ruled by God and the earth belongs to the authority of mankind. The way in which we operate in the heavens is different than that of the earth. God is the God of the heavens and He alone allocates sovereignty or the right to operate in the cosmos. To operate in the second heaven, there are rules that one must learn and follow. The highest heavens are God's dwelling place, and on His own authority, He grants certain members of His family operational functions in the heavens.

I'll never forget that day in 2007, when in a deliverance session, a fallen angel from the highest of the four dimensions in the second heaven, who presided over the Masonic Lodge in the United States, called the "glorious one" came down. He was under orders from God the Father to make two decrees. Those two decrees were from the Word of God. He said, you better watch how you talk to me, and you better pray! The "glorious one" was saying from scripture, Jude 8, not to revile or slander angelic majesties, and as far as prayer, Matthew 17:21 and Mark 9:29.

WE, IN OURSELVES OR IN CHRIST, HAVE NO AUTHORITY TO REBUKE SATAN OR THE FALLEN ANGELS SINCE THEY ARE IN THE HEAVENS.

I have encountered thousands of fallen angels since that day. After those many encounters, I found that Jesus from His incarnate position did exactly what I was led to do. With the Fallen, I deal with them from the Word of God; using 'it is written'. To take this revelation to the next level, we must look at Zechariah 3:1-7(NASB):

Then he showed me Joshua the high priest standing before the angel of the Lord, and Satan standing at his right hand to accuse him. The Lord said to Satan, "The Lord rebuke you, Satan! Indeed, the Lord who has chosen Jerusalem rebuke you! Is this not a brand plucked from the fire?". Now Joshua was clothed with filthy garments and standing before the angel. He spoke and said to those who were standing before him, saying, "Remove the filthy garments from him." Again he said to him, "See, I have taken your iniquity away from you and will clothe you with festal robes." Then I said, "Let them put a clean turban on his head." So they put a clean turban on his head and clothed him with garments, while the angel of the Lord was standing by. And the angel of the Lord admonished Joshua, saying, "Thus says the Lord of hosts, 'If you will walk in My ways and if you will perform My service, then you will also govern My house and also have charge of My courts, and I will grant you free access among these who are standing here.

The one who reveals the vision to Zechariah is not the interpreting angel from the heavenly realms, but the Lord Himself. But, this celestial angel was high enough in the angelic order to interpret for Zechariah, that Joshua indeed was in the courtroom of God. Joshua the high priest was standing before the court and the Judge of all the universe, God!

Joshua is in God's court, and Satan is at his right hand accusing him. The right-hand reveals that Satan has information, Joshua's sins, that has given him the legal right to accuse.

Joshua is an official and representative of God's people. Joshua is in the highest of courts, and this is seen through the choice of Jerusalem, the holy land! This is a territorial and or national case. Notice this, Satan has a cause; the condition of Joshua and God's people. Yet conditionally, we all have the fallen nature, the flesh.

GOD IS THE ONE WHO WILL JUSTIFY US AS WE ABIDE IN CHRIST JESUS.

Let me go deeper then, to bring out the real meaning! The accusation was not that Joshua was sinful, which he was, but because of the sinful nature, the struggle was over if he could operate in God's courts! If you ever have encountered this type of spiritual warfare, you would know that the accusations or allegations are always according to the fallen nature and not our position in Christ. Through this fallen nature, we give the fallen angels the right to accuse. God is the one who will justify us as we abide in Christ Jesus.

Why did this happen to Joshua, it was God's time for restoration! It was God who decided to bring together and convene court. It was God's prophetic time clock, and the time had come. Let us look at the natural courts, which reveal different courts in heaven or the spirit realm. Again, spiritual warfare has proven this to be true! Most who write about the courts of heaven do not have thousands of encounters against the fallen angels, and so do not have adequate experience to write about the way in which God deals with the fallen angels through the many-leveled court system. The courts of heaven are for the fallen angels, but demons are on the earth; we must expel them.

Civil courts are where a plaintiff may sue a defendant. In civil court, anyone can file a suit with or without cause. They can walk into the courthouse with a filing fee and file a petition with the court and ask for the defendant to be served with process. This forces the defendant to file an answer to the suit or run the risk of a default judgment. My point here is that there are civil suits brought against us personally by fallen angels. These are personal accusations that are filed according to the fallen angel's level of rank and jurisdiction. In most cases, it will also include the iniquities of the bloodline. Remember, each court has a jurisdiction. Those jurisdictions are leveled in the petition. Simply put, fallen angels have territorial spheres of rule and that is seen through their accusations. We must know exactly what the personal charges are! If I leave it to a dream, word of knowledge or a prophetic word, scripture tells me that I only get part of what we are being accused of; 1 Corinthians 13:9.

In criminal court, the allegations must be brought before a grand jury to decide if there is probable cause. The grand jury is God's ruling council. This is seen in Psalm 82:1, where Elohim is used twice. First of God in the Hebrew grammar of singular verbal form "stands." The second must be plural, since the preposition in front of it, "in the midst of."

The preposition calls for a group or an assembly. Look at Psalm 82:1 closely:

> *I have said, "You are gods [elohim], and sons of the Most High [beney elyon], all of you.*

In criminal court, in most cases, the subject will be the sins of mankind in that territory. Each territory ruled by a fallen angel has a criminal court and a grand jury.

Let us take this revelation one step further! The burden of proof in a civil trial is the preponderance of the credible evidence, and the plaintiff only needs to prove 51 percent negligence on the defendant's behalf. We are represented by Jesus, 1 John 2:1, our advocate, so we are vindicated when we can prove our position in Christ 51 percent.

It is harder in a criminal trial. We must prove mankind's innocence beyond a reasonable doubt within that fallen angel's territory. There cannot be cause for doubt. The higher the fallen angel, the greater his sphere, and the greater proof needed for innocence. There are more sins to account for. With that said, fallen angels look at mankind as a whole, social groups, and hold mankind accountable. This is why those who talk about freeing social

WE MUST PROVE MANKIND'S INNOCENCE BEYOND A REASONABLE DOUBT WITHIN THAT FALLEN ANGEL'S TERRITORY.

groups or territories is complete falsity; a dream without true revelation.

Let me give you an example of apostolic dominion and the true freeing a social group; in the 1990's, Guatemala experienced an outpouring of the Holy Spirit. Another example was the Welsh revival in 1904. Sin in those territories dried up. Jails, clubs, drugs, places of sin were no more! Even the produce grew larger than normal size. People came and repented of sin and encountered the Holy Spirit. Righteousness started to reign! As righteousness started to reign, the fallen angels in that territory lost legal rights and power through sin. The prayers of the people and those who moved in power within the fallen angel's territory had gained rights by God, so the fallen angels were restrained, and forbidden, by a judgment, to bind the minds of men. This is how it starts, prayer and evangelism, with the demonstration of the Holy Spirit's power. To push through the resistance with the gospel and prayer. Back to the courts, we can be accused in either civil or criminal court. It is also important to know which court, civil or criminal, that we are being brought to trial in.

IF YOU HAVE THOUGHTS LYING THAT YOU WILL NEVER ACCOMPLISH GOD'S REVEALED PLANS FOR OUR LIFE, YOU ARE BEING ACCUSED.

In deliverance, when God brings down the fallen angel, the minister needs to find out if its criminal or civil. If its criminal, it will be according to what we and our bloodline has done through iniquity, coupled together with the sins of society within the fallen angel's jurisdiction. If it is civil, usually it is according to what we've done personally, our bloodline and or what we have done to others. Put simply, which court are we in, civil or criminal? What is the jurisdiction of the fallen angel?

This was a criminal case against Joshua and Israel. The iniquities in Israel's bloodline. Joshua's right to represent Israel. Joshua was engaged in his priestly duties in the Temple when he found himself the target of Satan's accusations. The right hand is a position of power, but it is also a position of the prosecutor in a lawsuit (Ps 109:6), but it is also a place of the advocate for the defendant (Ps 109:31). In the overall view, God's house is the creation, and within creation there are many courts. Which dimension of the four? What is the district? And, what's the case, civil or criminal?

Joshua would have free access to God's angels who stand as witnesses within each court. The condition was that Joshua would walk in God's ways and serve Him!

One more thing before we move on! How can you tell if you are being accused by the fallen? It is discernible through our thought life. If you have thoughts lying that you will never accomplish God's revealed plans for our life, you are being accused. The Fallen resist what is written in heaven about our life. Demons drive us to choose certain sins. We feel in the body that sin. These feelings reveal demonization. In most cases, the sin reveals the demon. But the fallen angels are different! They resist God's will for our lives through mental torment. The person never feels in the body, only the mind. They also resist us in accomplishing God's will through mental warfare, whether us personally or through willing mankind.

Let me give you my personal example! There was a truly high-level prophetic person who revealed through a prophetic word God's will for my life. That is when the accusations from a fallen angel started. This fallen angel was over my bloodline. I was being accused personally and generationally. At times these thoughts came in series and would last for days at a time. It was so intense at times, that I made a duplicate cassette recording of the prophetic word, thinking I might wear out the one recording I had. I also would play it two or three times a day during these mental attacks. This is what I believe was happening to Joshua. Whenever there is resistance whether it is mental, personally or through humanity, we must consider the fallen angels who govern this evil age.

EVEN THOUGH POWER MINISTRY IS TAKING PLACE; FALLEN ANGELS ARE STILL ABLE TO CAUSE PEOPLE TO MISUNDERSTAND.

> *And even if our gospel is veiled, it is veiled to those who are perishing, in whose case the god of this world has blinded the minds of the unbelieving so that they might not see the light of the gospel of the glory of Christ, who is the image of God. (2 Corinthians 4:3-4 NASB)*

Most theologians hold to the view that it is those who are lost, that Paul is talking about. Yes, that is true and obvious. But, it is deeper! He was talking to those who were Corinthian believers, and they were attacking his authority and honesty. Bringing charges of deceitfulness and underhandedness. Paul's character and his ministry were under attack. A territorial spirit was influencing the minds of those believers to discredit Paul so that the things that bring glory to Jesus would be suppressed.

Second Corinthians 4, Paul speaks of territorial fallen angels and one of their functions was to block the spread of the gospel. The Greek word 'veiled' is to hide or to keep secret. Have you ever heard of the saying, "hidden in plain sight?" This is what it means; disguised so well you can't see it even when looking straight at it. Even though the gospel is being preached openly and power ministry is taking place; fallen angels are able to cause people to misunderstand the value of what is taking place.

When a deliverance minister starts to cast out personally or corporately, this is when the fallen angels are most active in people's thoughts and ideas, working to control their reasoning, causing negative judgments and finally rejecting what is taking place. Anyone with any spiritual understanding knows that deliverance cannot take place unless God is doing it.

Mankind has been called to preach the gospel, bringing glory to God as Christ Jesus is being lifted up. It is an amazing thing that God in His wisdom has allowed the fallen angels the power to veil humanities minds and hearts. But this is the power of free will. To change one's mind or not! To look at something intently or not! The power of the choice!

How do Satan and the Fallen veil the gospel in other ways? First Corinthians 15:56-57 gives an overview. Paul says the first step is the law, the Word of God. It is our choice to live under God's law or live lawlessly! The first step is to question God's Word. The Fallen deceive and want us to choose what they did; to follow our own set of standards! We know the rebellion took place before the fall of humanity. Jesus disclosed the power of agreeing with the Word when He said to Satan during the temptation, "it is written." So by nature, we are rebels, like the Fallen, and have that Satanic nature in us. Our sinful nature seeking freedom from God by questioning God's Word.

Second, sin is a power! If it is a power, someone must hold that power. So sin is a spiritual person with power. The bible clearly teaches that either righteousness or sin will be obeyed. So if sin is a person and power, so is righteousness a person and power. That person is Christ Jesus!

Third, sin brings forth death. This is the result of those who willfully deny the gospel, live independent of their Creator, and live for the power of sin. Living for the desires of the flesh! They are walking zombies! When we speak of power, authority comes to mind!

THIS IS WHAT WE FACE AS WE GO INTO CITIES. A HIGHLY STRUCTURED WELL ORGANIZED FALLEN ANGEL ORGANIZATION.

Let us look at authority and power! Before anyone can rightly operate in a system of authority, we must know our parameters and restrictions. Authority, even in worldly systems, has parameters. Authority is the Greek word 'exousia', it refers to the right to use power, to take action, to issue commands, and to respond in obedience. This is key in using the power the right way; it takes understanding! If I don't know or come into a revelatory understanding, I cannot command with power because I don't understand the sphere of authority I need to operate in.

To operate with authority, we need to first understand whose authority we function under and to what level. Second, we must recognize and submit to authority over us. Third, we must understand the boundaries of our authority. Fourth, as we obey the first three listed, it is revealed to us that authority grows. Much like being promoted through your job. Fifth, we must learn the rules of engagement so that we don't get in trouble. Much like the workplace, we can get in trouble if we go beyond our job description. I see many believers misusing God's authority. Falsely making claims they understand very little of. Have you ever heard a believer say, the devil has no power over me. Not realizing that the devil's authority and power over them is sin.

Through our position in Christ Jesus, we have been entrusted with that same incredible authority. The reason most believers don't move in that kind of authority is that they lack understanding. They lack rules of engagement! They spend very little time seeking out the secret powers of evil, and how to defeat them. I'm talking about spiritual warfare. The reason everyone is not healed is that most don't teach and put into practice what is required to bring healing. Using authority correctly is not doing something in advance and then asking God to back you up. It is understanding the rules of engagement; whether it is healing or deliverance. How did Jesus move in such great authority?

> *So Jesus answered them by saying, "I assure you and most solemnly say to you, the Son can do nothing of Himself [of His own accord], unless it is something He sees the Father doing; for whatever things the Father does, the Son [in His turn] also does in the same way (John 5:19 AMP)*

Jesus explains proper authority in John. Many times I sense a corporate move and at other times, I sense nothing. Yet, if I visually see the power start to manifest and I feel nothing, I engage. Whether I move in faith or by unction, my point is that we all operate under someone's authority.

Since Satan is a fallen angel and has authority over evil in this age, he must delegate his authority. The fallen angels by way of delegated authority, have power. In Second Thessalonians 2:9, the Bible says, "The coming of the lawless one is according to the working of Satan, with all power, signs, and lying wonders." Satan has all power in the realm of sin. Through the many different realms of sin, he and the Fallen move in power. Paul says in this very chapter that the mystery or the secret power of lawlessness or sin is already at work. My additions. Paul says the Fallen can do miracles! Ask a Shaman or someone from the New Age movement if their god, the fallen angel, their spirit guide, can do a false miracle or false prophecy.

Lawlessness will stay hidden until something brings it out into the open. Deliverance brings the secret power of lawlessness out into the open and exposes its work. Power is a person! God is a person, and He has power. Deliverance ministries bring the work of demons and fallen angels out into the open, revealing their evil work through sin, sickness, infirmity, disease, and poverty.

> *When He had disarmed the rulers and authorities [those supernatural forces of evil operating against us], He made a public example of them [exhibiting them as captives in His triumphal procession], having triumphed over them through the cross. (Colossians 2:15 AMP)*

Paul tells us how to handle territorial spirits or fallen angels. First, they must be disarmed. Second, we must spiritually recognize what is operating against us. Third, we defeat them by exercising the work of the cross in all its righteousness. The fallen angels and the demons who work for the Fallen must be made a public example of. This means exposing the works of darkness through power ministry. In so doing, not only do we learn how evil works, but we grow a deeper understanding of who Jesus is. By defeating the multi-tiered kingdom of darkness the way Jesus did, we learn authority.

For we do not wrestle against flesh and blood, but against principalities, against powers, against the rulers of the darkness of this age, against spiritual hosts of wickedness in the heavenly places. (Ephesians 6:12 NKJV)

My expanded version of Ephesians 6:12 says this: For our wrestling match is not against flesh and blood [contending only with physical opponents], not against persons with bodies, but against cosmic powers or fallen angels within four levels of the celestial realm who rule in various areas and in descending orders of authority. Against world dominators of this present evil age, and against spiritual forces of wickedness in the heavenlies who have tiered authority.

This pictures a very highly structured organization of levels and grades according to numbers within a hierarchy who are well organized as a kingdom of four different dimensions in the second heaven. These different kinds of fallen angels within each of the four dimensions have descending orders of authorities and different rulers and sub-rulers according to their grade and number. These fallen angels are responsible for different areas of authority in the second heaven and rule over the earth through the minds of mankind.

Let us look at the fallen angels in action, Acts 14. Barnabas and Paul went to Iconium and preached the gospel in a Jewish synagogue. God moved so powerfully through the effectiveness of the message that a great number of Jews became Christians. Here is where the fallen angels resist the gospel or I could say, blinded the minds of men. Some of the Jews refused to believe, the Fallen influencing the minds of men. The power of the choice! The fallen angels even stirred up others and poisoned their minds against Barnabas and Paul. Notice Paul and Barnabas continued to preach boldly, and God did miracles. We read a little further, the people of the city became divided; some sided with the Jews and the others sided with the apostles. Two invisible kingdoms at war! The unbelieving Jews and Gentiles plotted to mistreat and stone the apostles, so the apostles fled. When the gospel is preached, and God's power is involved, the Fallen resist. In deliverance language, the fallen angels caused half the city not to believe and stirred up the demons in those people to mistreat, speak ill of, and plot to stone Barnabas and Paul. The book of Acts is full of examples of how the fallen angels have the power to blind the minds of men.

Our wrestling match is not against or contending with people only, but against the cosmic principalities in the celestial realms who rule in various areas and their descending orders of authority. Who command the terrestrial demonic forces in countries, states, cities, institutions, organizations, people groups, and families.

This is what we face as we go into cities. A highly structured well organized fallen angel organization. These territorial spirits have the authority and power not only to influence the minds of humans, but give orders to harass, oppress, and possess mankind through demonization.

Ephesians 2:1-3 states that all mankind walked and behaved according to the fallen angel's values, beliefs, and morals. A desire for independence from God and lawlessness. This scripture states that the prince of the power of the air exercises administrative control over the earth through choices of disobedience; lawlessness. This is the power of the kingdom of darkness. It is the rejection of belief in the truth. Notice Satan working in and through the rebellious. Satan here is not only a person but also a metaphor for the fallen angels. What Paul is referencing is an evil age filled with every kind of lust of the flesh. It is an influence to indulge in the desires of the satanic nature. It is the result of our obedience to the lawlessness of the fallen angels and the sinful or satanic nature, that brings the wrath of God.

CHAPTER NINE

POWER ENCOUNTERS EXPLAINED

There are many things that you will read in this book that are commentaries on biblical definitions, but nothing expounded on as deep as this. Most writers have not experienced deliverance and healing (like the ones listed in this book) that could move them to write from a biblical definition. With more than 20 years of experience, and thousands of power encounters, it is my goal to write commentaries from my own experiences with the Holy Spirit from definitions found in the Logos Bible Software Program.

I could have written about legal rights, inner-healing, strongholds, curses, and witchcraft covenants like most writers do – not using scripture as a format. Nothing is wrong with those, in fact, I praise God for all the deliverance authors who teach a well-balanced approach of non-confrontational and confrontational spiritual warfare. I have a strong desire to uncover scripture as the supernatural is taking place and bringing correct definitions to light. Not only bringing clarity but explaining and clarifying the definitions of supernatural transactions that happen within the power ministry. The things I am writing about are power encounters that I have experienced according to the scriptures. Many times the Holy Spirit would speak scripture to me during a power encounter, which would inspire me to search deeper into that definition to discover more about the supernatural events that were taking place. Those experiences would never be uncovered except through power encounters. I must cover steps to healing, deliverance, inner-healing, curses, strongholds, witchcraft covenants and more, but only as the selected scriptures reveal.

We will start in the deep end, specifically in Mark 5 when Jesus confronts the demoniac. Why is this the deep end? Because it is in this book that the rubber meets the road, so to speak. In John 5, Jesus says, "I tell you the truth, the Son can do nothing by Himself; He can do only what He sees His Father doing, because whatever the Father does the Son also does" (NIV). This is a powerful rule for the supernatural; o obey the leadings, unction, thoughts heard as voice, audible voice, and the knower will lead to power encounter through faith.

The Gerasenes was located southeast of the Sea of Galilee and was one of the most important cities in the region.

I HAVE A STRONG DESIRE TO UNCOVER SCRIPTURE AS THE SUPERNATURAL IS TAKING PLACE AND BRINGING CORRECT DEFINITIONS TO LIGHT.

According to various manuscripts, it was called both Gergesenes and also Gadarenes. Gadara was a city of Ten cities as verse twenty explains.

It was a Gentile region to which the Father had sent the Son of God, to this man who was in torment (4:35). I see the value of every human soul first in these scriptures.

It was Legion and the demons that stirred up the destructive, suicidal bolt in the pigs. The stampede of the pigs reveals what had been going on inside the man. The torment must have been intense, for the man to try to kill himself – This torment is very common with those who cut themselves. The demons inside must torment unto blood for power. Witchcrafts ultimate power is the murder of a soul, blood power. These blood pacts attract high-level demonic spirits and fallen angels. At its core, these blood pacts are sacrifices during a witchcraft ceremony in which its rituals, oaths, pacts, and incantations (a series of words said as a spell or charm) are performed to attract or call on evil spirits. A spell is an enchantment with words and or deeds caused by witchcraft rituals.

Can you see this highly vexed bloody man? If he was like any of the cutters I've dealt with, his arms and legs must have been severely scarred. Most cutters have their cutting box like a heroin addict has their rig set. Cutters have their tools to alleviate the emotional pain that the demons have invested in them. Wherever you find emotional trauma or human hurt, you may find demons and dissociation. Dissociation is the splitting or fragmenting of the soul.

In Mark 4, Jesus rebukes the wind, and the sea calms down. On the surface, it looks like a miracle through faith, which it was, but it was also deeper! Rebuke means to express sharp disapproval and to reprimand for behavior and actions. So what did Jesus disapprove of? His own creation? No! On the surface, we understand the word as a natural storm or hurricane, but it is also defined as an atmospheric phenomenon. Winds can also be spirits! Jesus was on the Father's mission, all creation should have been in alignment. This storm came from another realm! This was a territorial fallen angel sphere of authority that Jesus and the ship had moved into. At times of deliverance, a supernatural phenomenon often takes place – lights turn off, objects start to move, and other things of the like. Jesus moved into the region of a territorial fallen angel who was high enough in the creation to stir up the wind, a hurricane, to make the sea impassable.

Once Jesus stepped foot on the land, the ruling demon who works for the fallen angel, the one who had stirred up the wind to prevent Jesus from coming, decided to confront Him. It was now Legion's fight! This should be learned early in spiritual warfare. After having worked in both realms for years, demonic and fallen, fallen angels do not come down in most cases unless God orders them down for judgment. It was the ruling evil demonic spirit Legion's responsibility to defend his legal territory on land.

As long as people continue to sin or allow sin in a region, the evil territorial fallen angel does not have to leave. Fallen angels look at humanity and human races as groups. Territorial fallen angels are structured in that manner. This also should be learned early in spiritual warfare. If an individual wants freedom, God will make the fallen angel come down to give that person and family up. But this only applies to those who are living for Jesus. As long as that family lives for sanctification, the territorial fallen angel cannot harass them, even if living in his sphere of jurisdiction. One last thing about fallen angels is that their names and functions are completely different than demons. Power encounters and the word of God have taught me that!

The first fallen angel I faced was called the "glorious one", and I later discovered he can be found in scripture. He was a high ranking archangel who has a throne in the second heaven. God had sent him down to let go of a woman and her bloodline. It took me by surprise because I had thought that Jesus had handled second heaven fallen angels. I was told by the fallen angel, the glorious one, "You had better watch how you talk to me, and you better pray!". (We will talk about what he meant in the next chapter, Further Power Encounters). The Holy Spirit immediately fell and started directing me to pray scripture. Later, I remembered Jesus' power encounter with Satan, when He was tested and was answering Satan's accusations with the word of God. This

AS LONG AS PEOPLE CONTINUE TO SIN OR ALLOW SIN IN A REGION, THE EVIL TERRITORIAL FALLEN ANGEL DOES NOT HAVE TO LEAVE.

format has been standard practice. The Father sends them down, I listen to the Holy Spirit, pray for the word, and judgment falls. Why do I never have to go into the courts of heaven? Because God's court is over all creation, my jurisdiction is on the earth. The Church's mandate is to subdue the earth as per the command to Adam. The demonic spirits work for the fallen angels, so whenever the Church is moving in the great commission, God will judge the Fallen.

Even some of the most conservative commentaries say evil spirits had entered the man's body and were controlling his mind, will, and emotions. This man was so possessed that he could no longer be part of the community. This is a stronghold! Today, that would mean institutionalized in some psychiatric hospital and heavily sedated with drugs. His dwelling place and permanent place of living were among the tombs or graveyard. Yet, this location goes a little deeper. It also includes a supernatural location by definition. Being among the dead, evil spirits are able to draw supernatural power from the earth amid the dead, which is rooted in witchcraft.

The word subdue means to tame, bring under control or to overcome something wild and uncontrollable. This man did not start out this way! Over time, demons such as fear, abuse, rejection, depression, anger, self-hatred, and witchcraft got hold of him. Not to say he had these demons, but a deliverance minister would suspect that these were there. My point is that most of humanity and even the body of Christ suffer from these demons. If these evil spirits have not entered your generation, believe me, they will try to target one of your future generations. I'm sure the demoniac said in the beginning, I can manage this. I can manage my sin. No one can manage an evil spirit who enters through transgression. Once an evil spirit is in someone, it must be expelled. There is no other way!

This possessed man would cry out in mental torment, screaming and howling with a harsh utterance and shriek. He would often babble or to talk rapidly and continuously in a foolish and confusing way. This is how the definitions describe him.

THE CHURCH MUST STOP DISTANCING ITSELF FROM THE IDEA THAT FALLEN ANGELS AND DEMONS PLAY ANY KIND OF A ROLE IN HUMAN BEHAVIOR.

It reminds me of some of the homeless men and women that I've done exorcisms on. They talked about hearing voices inside their mind and even outside their body. They could often be found talking to themselves in a confusing and incomprehensible way, carrying on conversations with the invisible. The first time I ministered to a schizophrenic, one who was on 8 different medications and still not in his right mind, the Holy Spirit told me to start casting out first! We see this with Jesus. This man's first strongman to go (with his kind or the evil spirits who worked for him) was schizophrenia. This brought the man to a place where things were much better. He could hear voices both in the mind and outside the body, but it seemed to him, to be at a distance. Then the Holy Spirit said, do it again, cast schizophrenia out of other parts of him, and this silenced the voices. What I mean by that is that schizophrenia came out of dissociated parts. The man had to be delivered from fallen angels and go through 6 more months of ministry, but within 3 months he was off all medications and had a job! Oh, what a trained believer can do with the Holy Spirit! The Holy Spirit showed me that I had to get the man's will back, not trying to overpower all his evil spirits. I have learned that the human will is our protection through choices.

Verse 15 says that this man was found dressed, no longer naked or disarmed, and in his right mind. Most believers think this man was set totally free, and while it does not say that it could have been. What we do know is that he was armed again, in his right mind, and free to choose between good and evil. Many times I have accused demons of making the person comment a particular sin, and the demons say yes, but the person chose, disarmed. Choices like unforgiveness, abandonment, rejection, fear, bitterness, anger, hatred, rebellion, pride, and depression injure us emotionally and are doorways for evil spirits. These choices also bring sickness to our bodies and are a torment to our soul.

In this showdown between Jesus and Legion, Jesus ordered the territorial demon (not fallen angel) to come out of this man. By close examination of the texts, Legion did not come out. Demons don't have to come out if they have legal rights, strongholds, and curses. Notice by the text, again and again, that Jesus interrogated Legion, not conversed with him. There is a clue in these scriptures on how the ministry session went. The man in some form of free-will ran to Jesus and fell on his knees in worship. This brought the demons up immediately! After thousands of exorcisms, I can see this plainly. The demons came up, Jesus interrogated, the man came back and renounced and repented. Legion and his kind lost their rights, begged again and again as his strongholds were torn down. Once the inner healing and demonic rights were removed, Legion came out with those that worked for him.

There is one more thing here, Legion begged not to be expelled out of the area. I have seen this many times, in fact, two weeks ago in Colombia, South America. I came across an evil spirit called Python. This was a witchcraft spirit rooted in divination and sorcery. The pastor of the Church said this spirit was regional, so I started a corporate deliverance. When I began the demon list and got to python, divination, and sorcery, most everyone in the church started manifesting, coughing, throwing up, and shrieking as these spirits came out. Python was a territorial demon and was in most of the people who lived in that city. So it was with Legion! I find most demons beg not to come out and go to the abyss or the pit. Demons don't want to go to the pit, which must be a very dreadful and tormenting place.

Summing this power encounter up, legal rights, strongholds, curses, and inner healing had to take place before evil spirits were cast out. The Church must stop distancing itself from the idea that fallen angels and demons play any kind of a role in human behavior. Does the Church put too much emphasis on problems of individuals as a result of the carnal nature or are evil spirits at work in devious and undetectable ways? I would submit to you, that everything that is good or evil has its source or origin in spirituality. The more I see rebellion in humanity, the more I see evil spirits at work.

In Mark 1:24, the demons referred to Jesus as Son of the Most High God. This shows us two things: One, they recognized Jesus as God's divine Son; Two, being an Old Testament saying, they had been working in humanity, even throughout the Old Testament. We must not leave out this one revelation – the demons knew that at the end of the world, all that is evil will be thrown into the lake of fire (Revelation 20:10).

Chapter Ten

Further Power Encounters

What most people don't see throughout the gospels and the book of Acts is how active the fallen angels are, and their continual resistance and influence in the minds of mankind. Authors write about Mark 5 and Legion, a territorial demon with many under his command, begging Jesus not to send them out of the region.

My encounters with Legion are as follows: Legion was assigned the task by the fallen angels over that geographical region to have every person demon possessed within that geographic jurisdiction. Legion, as the ruling demon (not a principality) of the Gerasenes, he was assigned also to bring all the inhabitants under the reign of each sub-ruling fallen angel. Each person living in the region of the Gerasenes was to be demon possessed and each person was to come under the control of the sub-ruling fallen angels and the ruling fallen angel. I have found this to be true of almost every believer.

When you have operated in both the Celestial realm for 10 years and the demonic realm for 20 years, you learn a thing or two. When I state "geographical", I mean the land, it's features, the inhabitants, and even the weather patterns and natures complexities. Geography has to do with fallen angels spheres of jurisdiction. There are communities, cultures, and even the economics involved. Some ministries call this strategic-level warfare. My definition is spiritual warfare from the second heaven involving fallen angels who rule, with sub-rulers responsible for geographical areas of authority who command demonic spirits to infect mankind. This is high-level spiritual warfare.

We see another example of the fallen angels at work in Samaria through a cultist named Simon Magus or Simon the sorcerer. He practiced the nine covenants of the occult found in Deuteronomy 18:9-12. The Bible states in Acts 8 that all the people in the city gave heed, saying, this man is the great power of God or the divine power. Simon amazed the people with his sorceries and his white and black magic which operated from or through the fallen angels in that territory. It was not a demonic power but from the second heaven. Here again, it affected all the people and the land they lived in. From

PRAYER AND SCRIPTURE TO GOD ARE THE ONLY WAY YOU HANDLE DIRECT, FACE TO FACE COMBAT.

the scriptural description, Simon seemed to operate from all the fallen angels in that territory. What I mean is this, he could draw evil energy and do evil signs and wonders to astonish mankind from whatever fallen angel.

As Paul and Barnabas traveled through the island of Cyprus, they met a Jewish sorcerer, a false prophet named Bar-Jesus. He practiced the magical arts, which were the nine covenants of the occult. Through the powers of the fallen angels who controlled the evil practices of the island, they were able to control the proconsul, the governing authority of Cyprus. We also see more fallen angels at work in Acts 16 and the Python spirit. In Acts 18, it is Diana. These are obvious strategic spiritual warfare encounters or encounters with second heaven fallen angels. I would like us to look at Acts 3 & 4 and read about a specific second heaven fallen angel encounter.

There was a man crippled from birth who was carried to the temple gate Beautiful. One must be careful not to read to much into scripture, but this could be a possible generational issue. The lame beggar would ask for alms from those who entered the temple. Peter and John are moved by the Holy Spirit, and a miracle happens.

This miracle gives the Apostles an opportunity to preach the gospel. Peter says that Jesus has risen and that mankind should repent and be converted so that sins may be blotted out. Are you catching

THERE ARE ANGELS ALL OVER THE EARTH, WAGING WAR IN THE HEAVENLY REALMS FOR CONTROL OVER THE COURSE OF THIS EVIL AGE.

this? A group of people, the gospel is preached, a miracle happened, and Peter and John are arrested on the orders of the high priest Caiaphas and the Sanhedrin. This is the second heaven at work. I will talk about this in more detail in my next book.

So what have I figured out? What do I know about the second heaven and the fallen angels? I know that there is a way or a protocol in how we exercise and operate in authority. Prayer and scripture to God are the only ways you handle direct, face to face combat. This is how we speak to the fallen angels. The Fallen must come down on God the Father's orders. We can't go up into the second heaven, this is as bad as slandering angels, fallen or not! Fallen angels do not possess. They call themselves Fallen because this evil age is fallen. Their names are completely different than that of demons. They have angelic names, and the ones who are of the highest order, take on the names of Jesus, like the first evil angel I encountered. He called himself the "glorious one." Fallen angels are not demonic spirits, they are the fathers of the Nephilim or the half breeds of fallen angels and women. Who the father of the fallen angel is determines the wickedness of each demonic spirit. Fallen angels have spheres of authority and have powers. They draw more power from the sins committed in the territory and on a continent throughout the evil age. They accuse mankind before God within their court system or the level of authority in the heavenlies. The accusations they make are according to the sinful nature, whether the person is saved or not. There are four main categories or divisions in the heavenlies or the second heaven: thrones being the highest, dominions second, principalities third, and powers fourth. Within each realm, thrones, dominions, principalities, and powers there are, as far as I know, different angels. This is just some of the things I've learned in second heaven spiritual warfare.

There are angels all over the earth, waging war in the heavenly realms for control over the course of this evil age. Evil, dark, fallen angels seek to influence the hearts and minds of mankind and in so doing, exercise power and authority over regions within each continent.

Then the Lord appeared to Solomon by night and said to him: "I have heard your prayer, and have chosen this place for Myself as a house of sacrifice. When I shut up heaven and there is no rain, or command the locust to devour the land, or send pestilence among My people, "if My people who are called by My name will humble themselves, and pray and seek My face, and turn from their wicked ways, then I will hear from heaven, and will forgive their sin and heal their land. Now My eyes will be open and My ears attentive to prayer made in this place. For now, I have chosen and sanctified this house, that My name may be there forever; and My eyes and My heart will be there perpetually. As for you, if you walk before Me as your father David walked, and do according to all that I have commanded you, and if you keep My statutes and My judgments, then I will establish the throne of your kingdom, as I covenanted with David your father, saying, 'You shall not fail to have a man as ruler in Israel.'" (2 Chronicles 7:12-18 NKJV)

We are reading God's conditional contract to Solomon and Israel. Notice how God focuses on His people, how he focuses on every Israelite! This is how the fallen angels see nations. They really don't focus on one individual but on families and groups of people. One fallen angel can control many families or groups. Notice how God wants His people to pray and stay in a continual attitude of repentance. If the Church is a praying Church, and God deals with mankind individually, as far as salvation, then we must evangelize to reach humanity. Prayer is the most important tool in second heaven warfare. Evangelizing is the next step to weakening strongholds of fallen angels. Personal deliverance is a must after salvation, water baptism, and the baptism of the Holy Spirit. Just a quick note: Some people can't receive the baptism of the Holy Spirit until they go through deliverance. This is usually due to witchcraft in the family history.

When the scripture says God will shut up the heavens and there will be no rain, the second heaven fallen angels are involved. How I understand it today is that God gives a verdict from the courtroom and the Fallen have legal rights. The same is with the locust and pestilence. The work of fallen angels is to steal, kill, and destroy!

The condition of God's outpouring and blessing is to be humble. The Bible describes humility as meekness, lowliness, and absence of self. The Greek word means lowliness of mind, so we see that humility is a heart attitude. Then the believers are to seek God's face and presence and then turn from wickedness.

"But if you turn away and forsake My statutes and My commandments which I have set before you, and go and serve other gods, and worship them, then I will uproot them from My land which I have given them; and this house which I have sanctified for My name I will cast out of My sight, and will make it a proverb and a byword among all peoples." (2 Chronicles 7:19-20 NKJV)

God says, if mankind turns away and abandons His commandments and the statutes which are the ways God has ordained mankind to live, God will uproot the people from the land. This rebellion is enticed by the fallen angels. It is important to note that all evil comes from the Fallen, and demons are their foot soldiers sent to tempt mankind.

Scripture shows us that if people rebel against God's ways of living, invisible spiritual forces will bring about significant destruction. This affects humanity and our environment.

Paul the apostle suggests this when he says that recognizing the difference between the visible and the invisible will keep us from losing heart (2 Cor. 4:16). In verse 18 of this chapter, we are to look at the things which are not seen. Most believers look at the things which are seen. Behind the suffering of mankind, the origin is the fallen angels.

PRAYER IS THE MOST IMPORTANT TOOL IN SECOND HEAVEN WARFARE. EVANGELIZING IS THE NEXT STEP TO WEAKENING STRONGHOLDS OF FALLEN ANGELS.

Hardship, distress, misery, adversity, pain, trauma, and sickness are the weapons of the fallen angels. In most cases, the demons carry out the afflictions. In 2 Chronicles, behind moral good, virtue, peace, love, compassion, and prosperity is God's grace to us. Prayer and evangelism are designed to transform nations. It is the other parts of the gospel that must be instituted within the Church.

From the life of Paul the apostle, we must recognize that the crucial battle for world evangelism is a spiritual battle. That the weapons of the fight are not carnal but spiritual on many different levels. With any battle, there must be intelligence. The more information we have concerning the kingdom of darkness and how it operates, the more aggressive the army of God can be. This is key in the overall battle plan. This is a secret to breaking the strongholds of evil over individual souls, cities, nations. The more geographical the battle, the higher fallen angel encountered, and the resistance faced. There are more troops to contend with in the battle. More second heaven fallen angels involved who are directing demonic spirits and influencing mankind not to humble themselves, pray, seek God's holiness, take on evil through spiritual warfare, and evangelize.

In Romans 1:18, we see another scripture passage on the visible and invisible realms. These are heavenly encounters explained through scripture.

Verses 18-32 show us how God releases the fallen angels to bring about the destruction of humanity. God will not overlook sin! A sin is a person, whether a demonic force or second heaven fallen angels. But it is the fallen angels who carry out the influence of ungodliness and unrighteousness and seal the deal with demonic possession through the choices of mankind. Possession is not total as some would suggest. Possession comes through areas of the mind, will, and emotions when they are surrendered to sin. Demon possession takes place in the body, and the demon's desires are warred for in the mind of their host. But the fallen angels suppress the truth and promote the lie, just as Satan did in the garden of Eden. This is the invisible war!

Paul reveals that God made the world to reveal His glory and power. God says this through scripture, that the things that are made reveal His glory. God discloses His invisible attributes, and they are clearly seen in the creation. This means that every human being was created to glorify God. This is why the angels were created before the creation of the world.

The fact is that creation became corrupt through the activity of the fallen angels. Influencing Adam and Eve's mind, caused them to choose disobedience to the Word of God. This false knowledge, I call it the lie, had an effect that brought about a change in their reasoning, which led to an action that had a lethal effect on humanity. Mankind changed gods and became worthless in their obedience to the fallen gods. With reasoning that has its origins in the knowledge of the fallen angels, mankind exchanged the glory of God for an image; a worthless idol in the visible, but a fallen angel in the invisible. Mankind worshipped and served the creature Satan and the fallen angels. Mankind crafted idols which fallen angels desired, as a representation of them and so they could unleash unholy power. Today, it is idols within the heart of mankind. Just to list a few, money, sport, pleasure, the willful cravings of this life. Again, it is mankind giving glory and honor to principalities, evil fallen angels, through actions.

Who are the fallen angels? The Bible calls them the sons of God. They are supernatural beings, angels who were created by God. They come from a supernatural region or realm. They are an entity, so they have a soul, free choice. Fallen angels are supernatural, created beings who have some level of deity (a god) depending on their class and order in which they were created. They have levels of authority according to four levels of hierarchy, their class within those levels, and the number of created order! They are not a demon, in any form! In most cases the word in Hebrew, Elohim, is used singular, referring to God the Creator. But in some cases, it is used plural, Elohim, referring to the angels. These divine fallen angelic beings are called "sons of God" (bene ha Elohim in Hebrew) in the Bible. These sons of God rebelled against God and His divine council. They left their position of authority in the heavenly realms, came to earth in order to corrupt God's creation. They did this by seeking strange flesh and deceiving mankind into worshipping them. These divine beings are more than watchers, which is only a class of many like Cherubim or Seraphim.

PRAYER AND EVANGELISM ARE DESIGNED TO TRANSFORM NATIONS. IT IS THE OTHER PARTS OF THE GOSPEL THAT MUST BE INSTITUTED WITHIN THE CHURCH.

The angelic realm is often referred to as heavenly hosts. This alludes to many different angels, as the Bible indicates, but not all inclusive as watchers. The definition of the offspring of the fallen angels are hybrids, these evil angels came to earth and mated with the women of mankind, this unholy union gave birth to what is called the Nephilim. These angels chose evil, saw and lusted after the daughters of man, and said to each other, let us choose wives from among mankind. In so doing, they had to pay the penalty of their abomination. The evil angels were reserved or kept in everlasting chains under darkness or bound with everlasting chains for judgment. Now most theologians will tell you that some of these angels are bound in some pit waiting for God's judgment at the end of the millennium. Spiritual warfare, which helps unravel or makes bound, Bible doctrine, says that these evil angels are bound to darkness, evil! They are not in some compartment in hell, Jude says they are irredeemably chained under darkness.

Through direct combat in spiritual warfare, the fallen angels are not sent to what the translators call hell or Sheol, but to Tartarus. Hell is a place of punishment for the dead and departed spirits, this is where demons are sent. Sheol an Old Testament word is the abode or residence of the dead – not of the body but the departed soul. Sheol in a few instances is translated pit. But Peter uses the Greek word Tartarus in 2 Peter 2:4 and so distinguishes a totally different place. The Greek word Tartarus refers to a special spirit prison where the fallen angels are kept in chains of darkness, as most definitions refer to. But in spiritual warfare against the second heaven fallen angels of all class, Tartarus is a place designed by God to send the fallen angels after mankind has them judged by God in His courtroom. Then and only then are they chained in the everlasting dungeon of Tartarus. These spiritual evil angels scream as you can visibly see the human body react in the natural to being chained hand and foot in the spiritual, and sent to Tartarus. This is an amazing sight to see!

There are four words translated for all evil. In Hebrew, Qeber refers only to the actual grave, physical burial. The Greek Gehenna refers to the fire of God's wrath which will destroy the wicked at the close of this fallen age. Then there is the Greek word Tartarus which refers to a special spirit prison where the fallen angels are kept in chains of darkness. In my next book, I will talk extensively about how they are judged. How to handle yourself in such a conflict. What actually causes God to send them down for judgment. How to handle the courtroom trial that brings God's verdict and judgment. How they are sent to Tartarus. Any non-confrontational deliverance does not send the Fallen to Tartarus but allows them to continue to influence the minds of men to sin and do evil.

Notes

Coming Soon

Exploring Secrets of the Heavenly Realms

Vol. 2

AVAILABLE ON AMAZON

Made in the USA
Columbia, SC
01 February 2019